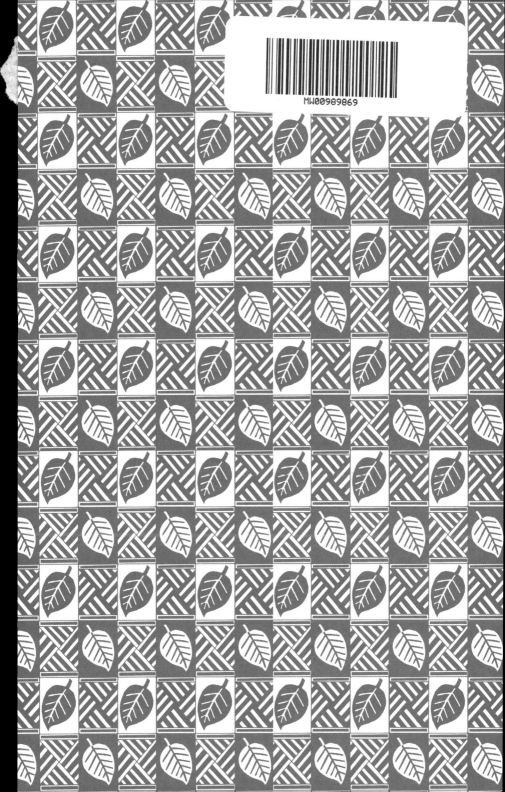

MW00989869

The Illustrated Story of England

The Illustrated Story of England

Christopher Hibbert
Illustrated by John Broadley
New chapter by Dr Seán Lang

The British
Melting Pot

⬥■⬥■⬥■⬥■⬥■⬥■⬥■⬥■⬥

The Shaping of
the Nation

The Struggle
for Power

•□•□•□•□•□•□•□•

The Rise and Fall
of Empire

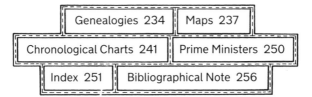

Author's Note

In the introduction to his short history of England published in 1947, Professor E. L. Woodward remarked that an attempt to cover so much ground in so limited a space was like trying to pack the Crown Jewels into a hatbox: 'you can do it only by leaving out the settings.' In this even shorter account of the most influential people who have lived in England during the many centuries outlined in its pages, and of the most important events which have happened during them, I have endeavoured to include as many of the settings as I could so that the book might be as lively as well as informative, even at the cost of omitting certain themes for which room might otherwise have been found.

It is intended as a generously illustrated introduction to the history of England for all those readers who have largely forgotten what they were taught at school, or whose history lessons touched upon only parts of the long periods covered here, as well as those looking for a readable book which will help to put the places they visit in their travels about the country into their historical context.

For further reference the chronological charts at the back of the book show what was happening in the world at large as the history of England unfolded. Specially drawn maps, showing all the places mentioned in the text, castles, cathedrals, country houses and battle sites, will also be found at the back of the book together with the genealogies of English monarchs and a list of Prime Ministers. Readers whose interest in England's history is stirred by this brief narrative are referred to the bibliographical note on page 256.

Christopher Hibbert, 1992

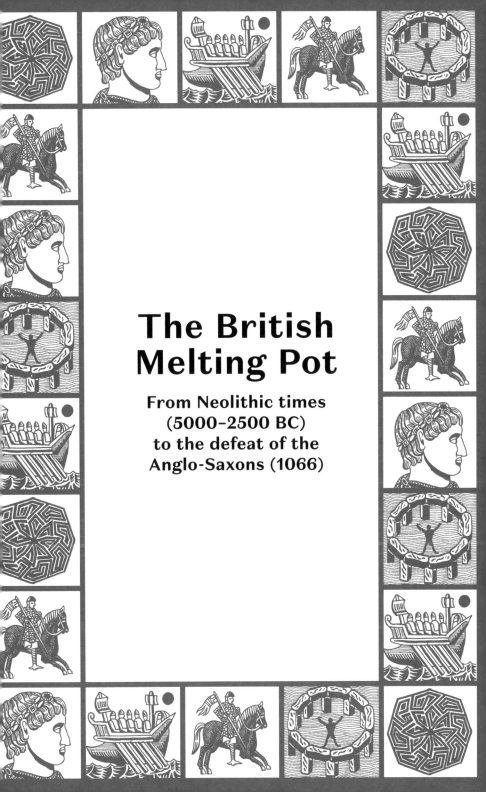

The British Melting Pot

From Neolithic times (5000–2500 BC) to the defeat of the Anglo-Saxons (1066)

5000 BC–55 BC
Natives and Immigrants

ne day towards the middle of the seventeenth century John Aubrey, a young law student at the Middle Temple, set out to explore the countryside around his father's estate in Wiltshire. Near the village of Avebury he came upon an extraordinary circle of huge stones which seemed to him to comprise an ancient monument 'as much surpassing Stonehenge as a cathedral doth a parish church'. Remarkable as the monument was and long as it had stood there, however, Aubrey's was the first detailed account of it. Even so, it aroused little interest. Seventy years later, in his *Tour through the whole Island of Great Britain* of 1724–6, Daniel Defoe did not consider Avebury worthy of remark; and, later on in the eighteenth century, when a local farmer decided to clear the ground for ploughing, several of the larger stones were pushed over into a pit filled with burning straw and smashed into fragments with sledgehammers. Stonehenge was treated less cavalierly, but it was not until recent times that any serious attempt was made to uncover the secrets of its history. Instead, tales were told of esoteric ceremonies, of priestly incantations, of human sacrifices upon the so-called Slaughter Stone.

John Aubrey discovered a circle of stones near Avebury

Since Aubrey's day, while scholars have stripped some of the more fanciful myths from these ancient stones, the reasons why they were so arranged remain a mystery, though the alignment of the Central Stone at Stonehenge with the Heel Stone – over which the sun rises on midsummer mornings – suggests a sanctuary connected with a sun cult. At least the monuments can now be dated with some accuracy. The Avebury stones were erected between 2000 BC and 1600 BC; the Stonehenge monoliths in at least five stages covering a span of nine centuries from about 2200 to 1300 BC. But of the people who placed them here, little more is known than of their purposes in doing so.

In the distant past, before the first monoliths were dragged across the open chalk down of Stonehenge from the mountains of Wales, that is to say seven thousand years ago, at the beginning of what was to become known as the Neolithic age, these and other areas of what is now England were occupied by roving bands of hunters who lived on the wild animals they could trap and kill, the fish they could catch in the rivers, or the wild plants they could pick. They grew no crops and had no livestock. Then, about six thousand years ago, these Stone Age hunters were joined by other peoples, immigrants from the Continent, small men and women, rarely more than 5 feet 6 inches in height, who crossed the sea in little skin boats, dug-out canoes and wicker-woven coracles, bringing with them a different way of life. They made clearings in the forests for their animals, grew crops, fashioned themselves axes and other tools from flint, baked pottery, and established meeting places and

Immigrants from the Continent brought with them a new way of life

tribal centres such as that at Windmill Hill near Avebury, whose summit was crowned by three concentric lines of earthworks. Followed by other immigrants, they developed the custom of burying their dead in stone tombs like that at West Kennett in Wiltshire, whose finds are in the museum at Devizes.

Among the new immigrants were the Beaker Folk who took their name from their distinctive bell-shaped drinking vessels with which they were buried in crouching positions in individual graves. These people, originally perhaps from Spain, came from the areas now known as Holland and the Rhineland, bringing with them a knowledge of working in bronze. They arrived towards the end of the late Neolithic period and the beginning of the period known as the early Bronze Age in about 2000 BC, and seem to have settled down amicably with the earlier immigrants. It was they who were responsible for bringing the immense stones from Pembrokeshire in South Wales for the second stage of the building of Stonehenge, probably shipping them across the Bristol Channel and up the river Avon on rafts, then hauling them up to the site from the banks of the river at West Amesbury on tree trunks serving as rollers.

Other smaller waves of immigrants followed the Beaker Folk; but the population of the island remained small and its settlements widely scattered until, for reasons not yet understood, in about 1600 BC thousands more people appeared. More and more settlements were built on the hills over the downlands; agricultural land was laid out in immense field systems surrounded by groups of hut circles. The population, it has been estimated, rose to about one million by 1500 BC when, at the beginning of the late Bronze Age, yet other immigrants arrived, bringing with them skills and ornaments of a quality which had never been seen in the island before and which were to be collectively known as the Wessex Culture. These newcomers were traders as well as craftsmen, builders as well as, when necessary, warriors. As the Beaker Folk had done before them, they turned their attention towards Stonehenge; and, in the third stage of its building, dismantled the circle of stones erected by their predecessors, then dragged eighty immense blocks of sarsen stone from the Marlborough Downs to set them up, squared and dressed with their shaped lintels, in the circle and horseshoe of trilithons which still stand today.

Diverse as the people in the island already were, their stock was to become more varied still when in about 800 BC, at the beginning of the Iron Age, other settlers arrived from the Continent, at first in small groups then in larger bands. These were the Celts, a taller fairer race than the people who had come before, members of tribes which had long been settled in present-day France, Belgium and southern Germany and which were now moving west, retreating from more warlike tribes harassing them from the east. According to Gildas, the Celtic monk who was one of Britain's earliest historians, the Celts were 'completely ignorant of the practice of war'. In fact, their fighting men were armed with iron swords and daggers and their chieftains drove two-wheeled war chariots which were buried with them.

In the country they called Albion they built fortified hill forts with turf and stone ramparts, good examples of which can be seen at Maiden Castle in Dorset – which covers 115 acres and at one point has no fewer than eight lines of defence – and Cadbury Castle in Somerset, formerly a Neolithic settlement and occupied almost

**Immense stones were brought from South Wales
to West Amesbury to build Stonehenge**

continuously for forty centuries. From such forts as these, and from
other strongholds protected by water rather than ramparts – like
Glastonbury which stood on an island surrounded by swamps –
Celtic tribesmen raided nearby settlements and carried off prisoners
as slaves.

But the Celts were not essentially a bellicose people; even their
chieftains seemed to have preferred hunting to war, while lesser
men and women devoted their energies to husbandry. They were
practised farmers, dividing the land into square fields separated
by banks and working the earth with small ploughs drawn by oxen.
They grew oats and rye, wheat and barley. Corn was ground in
handmills for bread; and the alcoholic drink known as mead was
made from water and fermented honey. They lived in round huts of
wood and clay-covered wattle with thatched roofs. Both men and

women wore brightly coloured clothes, red being a favourite colour, the material being dyed with a substance extracted from cockles. They had shoes and sandals of leather; and those who could afford them wore finely crafted ornaments and jewellery, brooches, bracelets, necklaces and rings, some of them made by their own people, others imported – together with glassware and wine – from foreign lands to which hides and slaves, cattle, dogs and minerals, tin from the mines of Cornwall, iron from Sussex, as well as gold and silver, were sent in return.

Among the most industrious and virile of the Celtic tribes were the Belgae who had begun to immigrate to Britain from the valley of the Marne towards the beginning of the first century BC. They settled at first in the south-east, where they soon became the dominant people in the area; and, as their coinage testifies, they established centres at Colchester, St Albans and Silchester. One of the most powerful of their chieftains was Cassivellaunus, uncle

The Celtic monk, Gildas

to Cunobelinus, Shakespeare's Cymbeline, who ruled over a large area north of the Thames in what is now Hertfordshire, Buckingham-shire and Berkshire.

Kings like Cassivellaunus were far from being the barbarians of Roman propaganda. They were skilled administrators, patrons of artists whose beautiful curvilinear, abstract art decorated not only war shields and the hilts of swords but the backs of bronze looking-glasses and the lids of jewellery boxes. Certainly, when they made their appearance on the field of battle, they presented an awesome sight in their chariots surrounded by warriors wearing no armour, their hair long, their naked bodies dyed with woad. Yet for most of the time their people seem to have lived at peace with one another, marrying not only within their own tribes but with descendants of men and women who had come to Britain long before them. They learned about gods and the transmigration of souls from the wise men, astrologers and soothsayers known as Druids who worship-ped and performed their rites in woods by the light of the moon beneath bunches of mistletoe clinging to the branches of oaks. According to Julius Caesar, the Druids offered up human sacrifices to their gods, sometimes single victims, at other times groups of men in immense wickerwork cages, criminals when these were available, slaves or poor men when they were not.

The Druids performed their rites in the woods by the light of the moon

55 BC–AD 450
Roman Britain

ulius Caesar, the great Roman general, invaded Britain for the first time in 55 BC, partly to gather information about the island of which so little was then known and partly to punish the Belgae who had helped their fellow tribesmen in their fight against the conquering Romans in Gaul, the land that is now France. He landed in Kent with several thousand men, although the soldiers in one of his legions had threatened to mutiny when told they were to invade the cold and misty northern island reputed to be full of savages wilder even than the Gauls. Strong tides prevented Caesar's cavalry from getting ashore; so, after some skirmishes in which the Romans took measure of the island which they were to call Britannia, he decided to withdraw. He returned the following year; and, although his sailors once again experienced difficulties with the treacherous waters of the Channel and several of his ships were badly damaged as they lay at anchor in a storm, he marched as far as Wheathampstead in Hertfordshire, Cassivellaunus's hill fort, which Caesar captured after fierce fighting. He then withdrew with hostages and prisoners, having extracted an undertaking from Cassivellaunus and other British chieftains that they would pay an annual tribute to Rome.

Julius Caesar's men invaded Britain in 55 BC

Caesar returned to Rome with the knowledge that Britain was far from being the primitive island of brutal tribesmen which the Romans had previously imagined it to be. It was not, however, until AD 43, after the death of the Belgic chieftain, Cunobelinus, that the Emperor Claudius decided to incorporate it into the Roman Empire. There was fierce resistance to the Roman legions which, having landed at Richborough in Kent, were brought to battle by Cunobelinus's son, Caractacus, by the banks of the Medway river. But, brave as they were, the Britons could not withstand the might of Rome. Defeated, Caractacus fled to Wales where, years later, he was captured and with his family taken in chains to Rome. After his defeat other British chieftains accepted the impossibility of successful resistance and submitted to the Emperor. Cogidubnus, chief of the Regni, did so, for instance, and was duly rewarded, having Roman titles bestowed upon him by the Emperor and accumulating great wealth.

The Iceni of East Anglia also submitted at first; but when their chief, Prasutagus, died in about AD 60, bequeathing his property to the Roman Empire jointly with his two daughters, his wishes were disregarded by the Romans, who refused to accept Prasutagus's widow, the tall, red-haired, harsh-voiced Boudicca, as queen. When she insisted upon the recognition of her rights and those of her family, she was flogged and her daughters were raped. The enraged Iceni, assisted by the neighbouring tribe of Trinovantes, swarmed down towards the Roman town of Colchester, massacred its inhabitants, sacked the recently constructed temple and other buildings

A Roman coin depicting Emperor Claudius

associated with the alien Roman rule, and routed the 9th Legion which had arrived from Lincoln too late for the town's defence. Then, led by Boudicca, the Britons turned south for the Thames and within a few days their rough and massive army was looking down upon the port of Londinium, then an undefended trading centre whose warehouses, shops and taverns, a few of ragstone and tile but most of wood and thatch, all lay open to attack. The destruction of the port was swift and complete. As at Colchester, its inhabitants were massacred and their buildings engulfed in flames. Boudicca's triumph, however, was short-lived. Faced by the power of a vengeful Emperor, there could be no final victory; and, rather than fall into the hands of her enemies, she took poison and joined the countless thousands of dead.

London was rebuilt, grew and prospered. By the middle of the third century, when it had become the administrative as well as the commercial capital of the Roman province of Britain, it contained perhaps as many as 30,000 people. Fifty years later there may have been almost twice that number, living in a semicircular area of 326 acres enclosed by three miles of strong stone walls, pierced by gates where the main roads entered the city, and strengthened

by bastions and towers. Elsewhere in Britain, as recalcitrant tribes were gradually conquered and pushed back towards the frontiers of Wales and Scotland, the Romans built other large towns, with temples and basilicas, barracks and public offices, amphitheatres, baths and workshops.

Most of these towns were arranged on the Romans' favourite grid-like plan which can still be recognized in the layout of the centres of Chichester (Noviomagus) and Gloucester (Glevum). In the north was York, then known as Eboracum, originally the head-quarters of the 9th Legion. On the northern borders of the Welsh Marches was Chester (Deva), headquarters of the 20th Legion. Other cities were developed on the sites of old British settlements. Among these were Lincoln (Lindum), St Albans (Verulamium) and Silchester (Calleva), whose Roman walls still stand in places up to fourteen feet high. Other towns were developed as spas, most notably Bath

Boudicca led an army of Britons against the Romans

Roman legions helped to establish towns across England

(Aquae Sulis) whose baths and temple, now fully excavated, were revealed when the city was rebuilt during its eighteenth-century heyday. Yet others were constructed upon virgin sites, such as, for instance, Exeter (Isca Dumnoniorum). Between these towns the Romans constructed a network of major and secondary roads, not always as straight as tradition would have them, but of remarkable solidity as the surviving road across the moors at Blackstone Edge, Littleborough, still testifies. From London, roads radiated all over the country along routes which for much of their length are still in use as modern thoroughfares: to the north by way of Watling Street and Ermine Street; to the east by way of the Colchester road; to Chichester in the south by Stane Street; to the west by the road that passed through Silchester then on to Cirencester (Corinium) and Gloucester.

Just off this road, at Chedworth, Gloucestershire, are the well-preserved remains of a Roman villa, one of many which Romanized Britons occupied during the days of the Empire. Over six hundred of these Roman villas have now been unearthed, ranging from quite simple one-story buildings to large houses of stone and slate, and splendid palatial residences like the villa at Fishbourne which was probably occupied by the Romanized Celtic King Cogidubnus. And, from the objects dug up on their sites and in their surrounding farms, it has been possible to reconstruct the pleasant life then enjoyed by the well-to-do under the protection of Roman rule. Togas seem to have been worn in the Roman fashion and shoes or sandals of leather. In cold weather, rooms – attractively furnished and handsomely decorated with porphyry and marble, bronze orn-

aments and terracotta figurines – were kept warm by heated flues beneath mosaic-patterned floors. In those rooms where meals were eaten there were blue and amber glass dishes and bowls, silver plates, knives and spoons, oil lamps and candlesticks. In bedrooms there were mirrors and boxwood combs on dressing-tables, ointment jars and scent bottles, ear-picks, skin-scrapers and manicure sets, pots of rouge, earrings and bracelets. There were pens and ink-wells for writing letters, dice and counters for playing games. Wine (better than the local fermentations) and olive oil were imported from the Continent, carpets from Egypt, silk, pepper and spices from the East. Latin was the official language; and most well-educated people spoke it as well as Celtic which remained the language of the poor, though many Latin words were incorporated into it.

For over three hundred years Britain remained a relatively untroubled outpost of the Roman world, the barbarians from beyond the frontiers of the Empire being kept at bay by forts and legions

The well-to-do enjoyed a pleasant life under Roman rule

Ornaments, pots and jars became objects of daily life

along coasts, at Branodunum (Brancaster) on the east coast, for example, and Anderida (Pevensey) in the south, and in the north by Hadrian's Wall, a great defensive barrier with a castle every mile, which was constructed on the orders of the Emperor Hadrian on a visit to Britain in about AD 121. Stretching seventy-three miles from shore to shore across bracken-covered moors from the Tyne to the Solway, it remains the most impressive surviving Roman landmark in the country.

Overrun and partially demolished by tribesmen from the north in 368, the Wall was again attacked in 383 and the sentries in its turrets and the soldiers in its forts were slaughtered out of hand. By now the Empire itself was beginning to crumble into ruins; and in Britain one legion after another was recalled to fight Rome's wars on the Continent until by the middle of the fifth century Rome's protection was at an end. The islanders were left to fend for themselves.

Hadrian's Wall was attacked from the north in AD 368 and 383

450–1066
Anglo-Saxons

he enemies of the Romanized Britons closed in upon them from every side. Fierce tattooed tribesmen rampaged down from Scotland; other marauders sailed across the turbulent Irish Sea in their light skin-and-wood boats called curraghs, massacring the farmers and fishermen along the western coasts; while, surging through the waters of the North Sea, came the shallow-draught ships of the Saxons, users of the *seax* or short-sword, and their northern neighbours, the Jutes, who fished and farmed in what is now southern Denmark, and the Germanic tribe, the Angles, who were to give their name to the English people.

Fair men with long hair and beards, clothed in thick, coarse shirts and trousers, in cloaks to which skins were sewn by their women to give them extra warmth when they were used as blankets at night, these raiders from across the North Sea carried iron-spiked spears, battle-axes and round wooden shields covered with hide as well as short-swords. Ruthless, violent men exulting in their animal energy, driving their victims before them like terrified sheep, as their war horns and savage shouts spread terror along the coasts, they pillaged and looted, raped and murdered, then sailed home again to their homes on the Continental mainland.

But soon, tempted by the good farmlands of Britain, they began to settle on the island, establishing small communities of rough huts around the wooden halls of their thanes.

In 446 the Britons made a final, forlorn plea for help from Rome; then, since no help was forthcoming, they turned – or so it seems from the confused and incomplete records of these times – to a powerful chieftain, Vortigern, who proposed bringing over as mercenaries a strong Saxon war party. These men, led apparently by two Jutish chiefs named Hengist and Horsa, established themselves on the Isle of Thanet, an area of rich farmland off the Kentish coast. At first all went well; but then the settlers, calling over friends and reinforcements, demanded more and more land and more generous payments until at length the quarrels between them and the Britons flared into open war. The British were defeated; the Saxons advanced; and, according to the Venerable Bede, the Northumbrian monk whose *History* is our chief source of knowledge for this period, the countryside and towns were alike devastated: 'None remained to bury those who had suffered a cruel death. A few wretched survivors captured in the hills were

Hengist and Horsa established themselves on the Isle of Thanet

King Arthur and his court at Camelot became a powerful legend

butchered wholesale, and others, desperate with hunger, came out and surrendered to the enemy for food, although they were doomed to lifelong slavery even if they escaped instant massacre. Some fled overseas in their misery; others, clinging to their homeland, eked out a wretched and fearful existence.'

This description is probably too highly coloured in its picture of woeful desolation; but certain it is that these were cruel times and that, rather than endure them, several families escaped across the Channel to the old Roman province of Armorica in the first of three stages of migration which eventually gave a Celtic language as well as the name of Brittany to this Atlantic peninsula of France. Other families apparently escaped to the west of Britain where a tribal leader named Ambrosius, evidently of Roman descent, offered shelter to the fugitives and to all those prepared to take up arms in defence of the old culture.

While the invaders continued to advance – one band of immigrants settling down in the kingdom of the South Saxons, which has given its name to the present-day county of Sussex, others establishing the kingdoms of the East Saxons (Essex) and of the West Saxons (Wessex) – further to the west along the borders of Wales and in Dumnonia, the peninsula occupied today by the counties of Devon and Cornwall, Roman Britain contrived to survive.

According to Gildas, a sixth-century chronicler who emigrated to Wales from Scotland where his father's estates were being constantly overrun by Pictish marauders, the Romanized Britons and British tribes threatened by the Saxon invaders flocked to Ambrosius's banner 'as eagerly as bees when a storm is brewing'. Presumably to protect themselves from the foreign marauders, and their cattle from raids by other British tribes, they built a series of earthworks, among them the Wansdyke, a massive ridge that stretches fifty miles from Inkpen in what is now Berkshire, across Savernake Forest and the Marlborough Downs to the Bristol

Channel; and, behind this earthwork, they seem to have withstood attack and even to have won the occasional battle. It was at this time that there arose the legend of the mighty King Arthur, champion of the British, noble knight and courageous warrior, who, as Ambrosius's successor, stood firm against his people's enemies. He fought twelve great battles against the Saxons, so the Welsh monk Nennius recorded, and 'in all these battles stood out as victor'.

Whether or not King Arthur lived it is impossible now to say. But that there came to the fore at this time a British cavalry leader of extraordinary prowess there seems to be little doubt; and of the power and fascination of the Arthurian legend and of his Round Table of heroic warriors there can be no doubt at all. Places named after him can still be found the length and breadth of the country: no other name in Britain is encountered so often, except that of the Devil. And from time out of mind the site of Camelot, King Arthur's court, has been identified as that of a yellow sandstone hill, Cadbury Castle, which rises in the heart of the quiet gentle countryside of Somerset. Here in recent years have been discovered fragments of pottery similar to those unearthed at Tintagel in Cornwall – where King Arthur is supposed to have been born – and splinters of glass of a type imported from the Continent in the sixth century as well as the outlines of what seems to have been a large feasting hall of the same date.

The last of the twelve victories ascribed by Nennius to King Arthur, 'Commander in the Battles', was apparently fought between 490 and 520 at Mount Badon which is believed to have been somewhere in Dorset or Wiltshire. This great victory, in which 'nine hundred and sixty men fell in a single onslaught of Arthur's', apparently brought peace for a time. But the encroachment of the Saxons across the island could not finally be resisted; and, before the end of the sixth century, Roman Britain was all but forgotten as Anglo-Saxon England began to take shape.

In the north the kingdom of Northumbria – one of the seven kingdoms, or Heptarchy established by the Angles and Saxons – extended its boundaries to the west; while, in the Midlands, the kingdom of Mercia assumed control over tracts of land so vast that by the end of the eighth century its ruler, King Offa – who built the

A portrait coin of Offa, King of Mercia

great earthwork known as Offa's Dyke along his western borders to keep out the Welsh – controlled for a long time virtually all central, eastern and south-eastern England. In the south the kingdom of Wessex took control of Devon and Cornwall as well as the lands of the South and East Saxons; and, at the beginning of the ninth century, under their King, Egbert, the West Saxons defeated the Mercians and even laid claim to authority over the lands north of the Trent. When the Northumbrians submitted to him and took him for their master in 829, Egbert could reasonably consider himself overlord of all the English.

The confederation of the different kingdoms was a very loose one, though; and Egbert's dominion over it was far from secure. He had no central government and no means of raising an army well disciplined enough to defeat England's new enemies from overseas. These were the Northmen, Norwegian Vikings and Danes, tall fair warriors and pirates, as hungry for land as the ancestors of the English had been four centuries before. At first they came as raiders in their high-prowed ships, ravaging and looting along the coasts, sailing home to winter in their fjords. But then they came to settle, sailing up the Thames, wading ashore in East Anglia and on the coasts of Northumbria, pagan men as ready to beat in the skulls of defenceless monks as to cut down the English farmers

who were assembled in their fighting forces known as *fyrds* to resist the approaches of what the Anglo-Saxon chroniclers described as the 'great heathen host'.

Christianity had come to England long before. Towards the end of the sixth century, Ethelbert, King of Kent, had ridden from his capital to the coast to meet Augustine, the Prior of St Andrew's Monastery in Rome, who had been sent by the Pope to convert the heathen English to Christianity. Afraid of the stranger's magic, the King had received him in the open air but, soon persuaded by his sincerity, he had allowed him to preach to his people and within a few months Ethelbert had become a Christian himself. He provided Augustine with a house for his followers in Canterbury and in 597 allowed him to be consecrated Bishop of the English.

Seven years later another missionary from Rome, Mellitus, had been established as Bishop in London where King Ethelbert had built for him a church which was dedicated to St Paul. But Mellitus had found the staunchly pagan Londoners far more intractable than Augustine had found the people of Kent and, after the death of his royal patron, the men of London had driven their Bishop out of the city gates and had returned to their old religion and their former priests.

Christianity, however, was gaining a strong hold elsewhere in England where the gospel was spread not only by missionaries from the Continent and their followers but also by Celtic missionaries from Scotland and Ireland and from the holy island of Lindisfarne which St Aidan, a monk from Iona, had been given by Oswald, the Christian King of Northumbria. The missionaries who came from Rome held that the Pope's authority was supreme, the Celtic evangelists that Christian belief did not require a final earthly arbiter. There was little agreement between the two factions who differed even upon the calendar that settled the date for Easter; so in 664 a conference was held at Whitby in Yorkshire where a house for monks and nuns had been founded a few years before by St Hilda, great-niece of the King of Northumbria. This Synod of Whitby decided in general favour of the Roman missionaries, foreshadowing closer ties with the Continent as well as the organization of the church into bishoprics, largely unchanged to this

The Northmen came in high-prowed ships

day, by such Christian leaders as the Greek, St Theodore, who was appointed Archbishop of Canterbury by the Pope in 668 and who called the first Council of a united English Church in 672 at Hertford, a demonstration of ecclesiastical unity that served as a model for a political unity not yet achieved.

As Christianity spread in England, churches were built all over the island. Most were constructed of split tree trunks which have long since disappeared but some were of stone, among them the original church of All Hallows by the Tower, the Northamptonshire churches of Brixworth and Earls Barton, and the little early eighth-century church of St Laurence, Bradford-on-Avon. Monasteries and abbeys were also being built, minsters, chapels and oratories; and as the Church received bequests and grants of land so its riches and influence grew year by year.

It was this increasingly Christian England, slowly evolving into a unified state, which was threatened by the Vikings and the Danes who, well established in the north, were by the middle of the ninth century posing a threat to the Saxon Kingdom of Wessex whose capital was at Winchester.

Here a remarkable young man had come to the throne in 871. This was Alfred, scholar, lawgiver, warrior and king, the first great statesman to emerge clearly from the mists of early English history. Of his physical appearance little can be said with confidence, but his biographer and friend, Asser, Bishop of Sherborne, painted a portrait of a man of exceptional gifts, devout and humane, devoted to the welfare of his people, as brave in battle as he was studious in scholarship, always careful to make the best use of his time so that he could continue with his studies and translations without neglecting the cares and duties of government, even inventing a water clock to help him in this endeavour.

In battle against the Danes at Ashdown in the Berkshire hills Alfred fought 'like a wild boar'. But, although his enemies were here defeated, the Danish incursions into England were soon resumed;

The Saxon church of St Laurence, Bradford-on-Avon, Wiltshire

and for a time Alfred, with a small company of faithful followers, was driven into hiding from the invaders on the Isle of Athelney in the Somerset marshes, moving 'under difficulties through woods and into inaccessible places' and giving rise to the famous legend that he sought shelter in a cottage where a woman scolded the unrecognized fugitive for allowing her cakes to burn by the fire.

Gradually, however, the number of his supporters increased; and by 878 Alfred was able to bring the Danes to battle once more and to defeat them decisively. He obliged them to remain within an area bound by Watling Street known as the Danelaw, and persuaded their leader, Guthrum, and several of his leading warriors, to be baptized as Christians. Taking advantage of the temporary peace, Alfred reorganized the *fyrd*, satisfying the complaints of men who had had to leave their farms for indeterminate periods to serve as soldiers; and he built up a strong navy to patrol the English Channel, forcing many would-be invaders to turn their attentions to northern France where their settlements became known as Normandy, the land of the men from the north.

Alfred, left for the moment in peace, turned his own attention to the restoration of English Christian culture, repairing pillaged churches, founding schools, setting scholars to work on the compilation of histories and the translation of texts, himself translating Bede's *History* – which celebrates the English people as a chosen race – grieving that men 'in search of learning and wisdom' had taken to going abroad 'when once they had come to England in search of such things', and looking forward to the day when 'all the youth now in England, born of free men, who have the means they can apply to it, should be devoted to learning'.

When Alfred died in 900, England was united as never before. By saving his own kingdom from the Scandinavian threat, he had given encouragement to others and had made the West Saxon cause the cause of England. His successors did what they could to continue his work. His son, Edward the Elder, as skilled a soldier as his father though not so dedicated a scholar, and his formidable daughter, Ethelfleda, wife of Ethelred of Mercia, who ruled that kingdom after her husband's death as 'Lady of the Mercians', kept the Danes at bay and constructed a system of defences by building *burghs*

or fortified settlements later to be known as boroughs, at strategic points, including Bakewell in Derbyshire, Tamworth and Stafford, Hertford and Warwick. Edward's son, Edmund, and his grandson, Edgar, gradually realized Alfred's dream of a unified England. The Danelaw was reconquered and in 973 Edgar was not only accepted as King of the English by Saxons and Danes alike, but also acknowledged as their overlord by kings in Scotland and Wales. During the reign of King Edgar, 'the Peaceable', between 959 and 975 there was a late flowering of Anglo-Saxon art and culture as well as an increase in the number of monastic houses for both men and women under the direction of St Dunstan, the scholar, musician and craftsman, maker of organs, bells and metalwork, who became Abbot of Glastonbury in 940 and Archbishop of Canterbury twenty years later.

King Edgar's descendants were, however, ill-suited to the task of defending England from renewed Viking invasions. His eldest son, Edward, was stabbed to death while he was still a boy; another son, Ethelred, who was crowned by St Dunstan when he was barely ten years old, was to be nicknamed 'the Unready' or 'the Ill-advised'. His willingness to buy off the invaders with bribes known as Danegeld angered his own people – who were heavily taxed to meet the cost of the payments – while failing to placate the Danes whose King, Cnut, took over the throne in 1016, incorporating England into a Scandinavian empire which included Norway as well as Denmark.

England prospered under Cnut, a firm, just ruler who took pains to conciliate the English, marrying Ethelred's widow and becoming a Christian, much to the pleasure of the monks of Ely who 'sang merrily as the King rowed thereby'. In his time Danes and Englishmen learned to live more amicably together – though the riches and power of Danish earls were the cause of much jealousy – and there began to emerge the counties of England as we know them today, an England divided into shires with shire courts and shire reeves, or sheriffs, responsible for administering laws as comprehensive as any in the early medieval world.

Most people still lived in country villages. But perhaps as many as ten per cent were now town-dwellers; and several towns, notably Winchester, Norwich and York were growing fast, as were ports

As legend goes, King Alfred — in hiding — sought shelter in
a cottage and was scolded for allowing cakes to burn

King Cnut, who incorporated England
into a Scandinavian empire

like Southampton from which the English exported their textiles, metalwork and foodstuffs, as well as the slaves and the hunting dogs for which they had long been celebrated. London's population had risen to about fifteen thousand.

It was natural that such a country should continue to attract the eye of foreign adventurers, despite the strong fleet that Cnut maintained by renewing the annual tax of the Danegeld. And after the short reigns of his two sons and the accession to the throne of Ethelred the Unready's son, the white-skinned, white-haired Edward – known because of his piety as 'the Confessor' – greedy eyes were turned to the kingdom of this indolent man who seemed more concerned with the building of a great Abbey at Westminster than with affairs of state.

As soon as it was learned that Edward was dying, no fewer than four men laid claim to the English throne, the King of Norway, the Duke of Normandy, and two brothers of Edward's Queen, Edith, one of whom, Tostig, the deposed Earl of Northumbria, was living

in exile in Flanders. The other of these two brothers was Harold Godwinson, the hereditary ruler or Earl of Wessex, who immediately took advantage of his rivals' absence from the country to have himself crowned in the new Abbey of Westminster on the very day that its founder was buried there.

Shortly afterwards Tostig's men invaded Kent, then sailed up the east coast to pour ashore in Lincolnshire. Defeated by local levies, Tostig retreated north to await the arrival of the King of Norway whose Scandinavian warriors were soon sailing up the Humber towards York. Informed of this second invasion, King Harold, who was in the south preparing to resist the expected attack from Normandy, rushed north, won a brilliant victory at Stamford Bridge and, leaving both his brother, Tostig, and the King of Norway dead, brought his exhausted troops back to the Sussex Downs to face the army of the Duke of Normandy who had landed his knights at Pevensey. On 14 October 1066 the two armies clashed in a hard-fought battle north of Hastings at Battle. Towards the end of the day Harold was killed, shot through the eye by an arrow as tradition supposes, then hacked to death by Norman knights, one of whom cut off his leg, an unknightly deed for which Duke William dismissed him from his service. Anglo-Saxon England perished with Harold's death.

**King Harold died at the hands of the
Normans at Hastings in 1066**

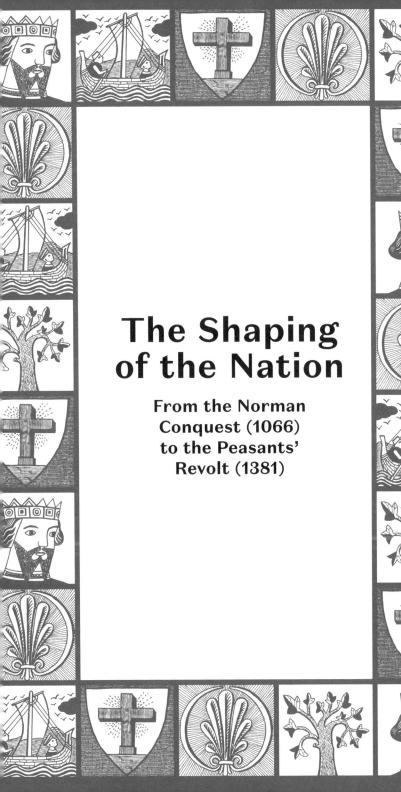

The Shaping of the Nation

**From the Norman
Conquest (1066)
to the Peasants'
Revolt (1381)**

1066–1154
Norman Rule

illiam, Duke of Normandy, the Conqueror, was then nearly forty years old; but it is difficult to say much more about him as a man with any certainty. He seems to have been about five feet ten inches in height, far taller than his minute wife, very strong and rather fat with reddish hair and a harsh, guttural voice. He was violent, domineering, calculating and avaricious, a man to fear. But he was abstemious, a pious Christian and, illegitimate himself, a faithful husband.

Vikings by origin and Vikings still by inclination – so holds one side in a continuing debate – he and his followers invaded England to deprive the island's people of their liberty, to kill their brave and noble King Harold, 'the hero and the martyr of our native freedom'. This was the testament according to Professor E. A. Freeman whose classic *History of the Norman Conquest* was published in five volumes in 1870–9. Another eminent Victorian, Thomas Carlyle, proposed a different interpretation: the Normans dragged us out of our primeval squalor. For what had the English been before they came? 'A gluttonous race of Jutes and Angles, capable of no great combinations, lumbering about in pot-bellied equanimity'.

Modern scholars rightly warn us to be on our guard against the misconceptions of this ancient and persistent polemical tradition, to recognize both the achievements of Anglo-Saxon culture and the benefits, as well as the ruthlessness, of Norman conquest.

Certainly William was not prepared to be merciful in his subjugation of his English enemies. His claim to the English throne, endorsed by the Pope, was genealogically stronger than the claims of his rivals; and he was determined to enforce it, to overwhelm all those who refused to recognize that his victory at Hastings had turned England into a Norman kingdom. For the moment this kingdom was far from secure: the Earls of Northumbria and Mercia both declined to submit, retiring to the north with the idea of proclaiming King Edward's young nephew, Edgar, as King Harold's successor; both the Archbishop of Canterbury and the Archbishop of York supported the proclamation of Edgar as Harold's rightful heir; King Edward's widow remained in control of the old West Saxon capital of Winchester; and the gates of London, the key to England's dominance, were closed against the Norman invader.

Understanding the importance of London, and accepting the difficulties of attacking so large and well-defended a town with the few thousand knights and archers he could lead against it, William decided to surround it. After setting fire to the wooden buildings in the suburb of Southwark on the south bank, he marched west into Berkshire, then north-east to Berkhampstead, devastating the countryside on the way; and once London had been isolated, his enemies, as he had hoped they would, submitted one by one, followed by 'all the chief men of London, and they gave hostages to him, and he promised that he would be a gracious liege Lord', a ruler who would treat them justly if they gave him their service. He entered London shortly before Christmas; and on Christmas day he was crowned King of England in Westminster Abbey where the shouts of acclaim were mistaken for calls for rebellion by the Norman soldiers on guard outside, who began killing English spectators. In places the fight against the Normans long continued; and William, who went back to Normandy three months after his coronation, had to return to England to put down revolts occasioned by the behaviour of the more rapacious of his barons,

William I, the Conqueror, decided to surround London

the powerful magnates, mostly brutal men who from such evidence as has come down to us appear to have been distinguished by moustaches of a monstrous size sprouting on either side of their iron nose-guards. On his return to England, William showed scant mercy: great tracts of countryside were laid waste, and towns as far apart as Exeter and Durham were made to suffer his wrath. In the north hundreds of square miles were devastated and whole villages destroyed. In revenge the English 'here and there lay in wait in woods and secluded places secretly to slay [the hated Normans] as opportunity might offer'. And in retaliation the Normans introduced a Law of Englishry which decreed that a corpse was to be presumed to be that of a Norman unless it could be proved to be that of an Englishman and, on that presumption, a heavy fine was to be paid by the village nearest to the place where the body had been found. No fines were levied for dead Englishmen. It was not until the end of the twelfth century that it became difficult to tell the difference between the one race and the other. By then they had 'lived so long together and [had] intermarried and become so intermingled' that contemporaries could 'scarce distinguish [any more] betwixt Englishmen and Normans'.

By then also the system of land tenure known as feudalism, already developing in Anglo-Saxon times, had become an accepted way of life. In accordance with this system, William had given his followers – Bretons and Flemings as well as Normans – large estates in England, all of which he was deemed to own personally, scattering the estates far and wide over the country, so that those who held them could not easily combine to rebel against the King. The barons and earls thus rewarded with this land became tenants-in-chief of the King, to whom they were obliged to swear loyalty and for whom they were required, when necessary, to perform military service with an appropriate number of knights. They were also required, when summoned, to serve on the Grand Council – the successor of the Witan, the council of the Anglo-Saxon kings – from which Parliament was eventually to develop. The tenants-in-chief retained as much of the land granted them as they wished, distributing the rest to knights as sub-tenants who in turn allocated parts of it to the men who actually worked the fields, either as freeholders or as serfs. These workers at the bottom of the feudal scale paid for their respective shares by serving their master when called upon to do so and by working in his own fields for stipulated periods. The free-hold tenants were allowed to leave the land if they wished and to settle elsewhere; but the far larger number of serfs or villeins were tied to the land of their lord and, in most cases, could gain their freedom only by paying for it or by running away to a town where, provided they had not been recaptured within four days, a court order would be required to bring them back into servitude.

In order to have a reliable record of all his lands, his tenants and their possessions and to discover how much they could be called upon to pay by way of taxes, William ordered the compilation of the inventory of his assets known as Domesday Book, now to be seen in the Public Record Office. From this it appeared that in 1086 about half the cultivated land in the country was in the hands of 170 tenants-in-chief, only two of whom were English barons; about a fifth was held personally by the King and most of the rest by bishops and abbots and other heads of religious houses who paid for it by their prayers or by paying scutage, a tax which lay landholders also came increasingly to pay in lieu of knightly service.

To the English serfs who lived within their shadows, the most obvious symbols of the power of their new landlords and masters were the castles that now appeared all over England, no fewer than five hundred of them within a generation of the Normans' coming. Others were to be built with every passing year; there were to be forty in Kent alone. The earliest of them were usually built of wood and quite simple in design. Constructed on an earthen mound, surrounded by a ditch, they comprised a tall tower enclosed on all sides by a palisaded rampart. The ditch was usually filled with water, and a drawbridge led across it to the castle's single gate. The great castle at Windsor and the Tower of London were first built in this modest way. As time passed, however, castles were required to serve not only as a means of overawing a disaffected and unruly people, as garrisons, supply bases and fortified centres of administration, but also as noble dwellings built of stone or flint or rubble faced with stone. They still had to be formidable fortresses with immensely thick walls, high towers and moats, and sometimes, as at Kenilworth, with a staircase on an outside wall leading to a heavy, well-protected door on an upper floor. But there also had to be sleeping chambers on the upper storeys, dining halls, chapels and, in the larger castles, a series of rooms known collectively as the wardrobe in which clothes were kept and valuable household stores, including expensive spices, were deposited in locked chests with jewels and plate. Such castles, ruined, restored or rebuilt, can be seen in every county, along the coasts at Dover and Bamburgh, in the west country at Launceston and Berkeley, in Sussex at Lewes and Arundel, along the Welsh marches at Ludlow and Chepstow, in Yorkshire at Richmond, in the Midlands at Rockingham and at Oakham where there is a fine example of a Norman castle's great hall built like a church with a nave and two side aisles, since masons had not yet mastered the craft of roofing a wide span.

Churches appeared even more ubiquitously than castles, for the population was rising rapidly and being divided into parishes, neighbourhoods within the counties which have survived virtually unchanged into our own time. There were relatively few people in the north which had been devastated so remorselessly in the years immediately following the conquest: in Yorkshire there were per-

The record of land known as Domesday Book
was completed in 1086

haps no more than thirty thousand people, and in the whole of the north probably no more than four people to the square mile. But few counties in the south had fewer than fifty thousand each. There were about seventy thousand in Devon, ninety thousand in Lincolnshire, and in Norfolk – the most populous county of all – nearly a hundred thousand. By the time of Domesday Book the population of England seems to have been approaching two million. Most of these people still lived in villages, since all but the five largest towns had less than a thousand inhabitants, and places where large towns were later to be built, from Portsmouth to Newcastle, and Liverpool to King's Lynn, were not yet even villages. Some towns, like Newbury in Berkshire, were recent Norman foundations; but most were Saxon towns, which had been growing slowly. St Albans, so populous in Roman times, and having well over eighty thousand inhabitants today, had just forty-six burgesses in 1086.

Yet, even in the north, builders were busily at work, erecting new churches, reconstructing Saxon ones, employing the style of architecture known as Romanesque with its rounded arches favoured by architects of the Roman Empire, square towers and plain vaulting. The west front of the parish church at Iffley outside Oxford is but one splendid example of Norman architecture at its most satisfying and robust, the nave of Durham Cathedral but one such nave in an

early English cathedral, the interiors of St Bartholomew the Great, Smithfield and St John in the Tower but two places of worship in London where the atmosphere of the Norman Church is powerfully evoked. Work on Durham Cathedral began in 1093. By then no fewer than fourteen of England's greatest cathedrals were already under construction; all the rest with one exception were started early in the next century. The one exception was Salisbury Cathedral which was not begun until 1220; but two miles north of Salisbury, at Old Sarum, a cathedral had been in existence since 1092.

William took a deep interest in the development of the Church in England, encouraging the efforts of the Italian-born Lanfranc – whom he had summoned from Normandy to install as Archbishop of Canterbury – to bring a characteristic Norman efficiency into the administration of ecclesiastical affairs and to take the English Church closer to Rome. Yet the King, for all his professed regard for the Pope and the Roman Church, took care to maintain his own independence: no bishop might visit Rome or even write to the Pope without his permission; no excommunications might be imposed in his large realm without his express consent. Although William's determination to be supreme in Church as he was in State often brought Lanfranc into dispute with the Pope, the Archbishop remained as loyal as he was devoted to the King; and when news was brought to him of the death of the Conqueror after an injury received while riding on the Continent, he was so prostrated by grief that his monks thought that he too might die.

Lanfranc's distress was exacerbated by his concern that the son whom William had chosen to succeed him was wholly unfitted for kingship. This son, also William and known as Rufus because of his florid complexion, was a short, fat, bull-necked man with a bitingly sarcastic tongue and a savage, bullying temper. He mocked the piety of churchmen, insulted foreign envoys and flaunted his homosexual tastes. One day he asked Anselm, the leading theologian of his day – who had been appointed Lanfranc's successor as Archbishop of Canterbury after a long delay during which the King appropriated the archiepiscopal income – what sin he would be condemning in his next sermon. Anselm bravely replied, 'The sin of Sodom.' The King laughed in his face.

While accepting money from malefactors who could afford to pay bribes to evade justice, William inflicted punishments on those who had offended against him with even greater severity than his father had done, blinding and castrating one rebel noble, and flogging the noble's steward by the door of every church in Salisbury before having him hanged. But to no malefactors was he more severe than he was to those who offended against the forest laws, the scope of which he much extended.

His father had earned widespread hatred for his strict imposition of these fierce laws and for extending the boundaries of the royal forests which included tens of thousands of acres of land, by no means all of it wooded, over which the King and his friends could hunt deer. To preserve this pleasure for himself William I had poachers blinded and mutilated, and even those who gathered sticks on royal land were savagely punished. Disregarding the objections and pleas of rich and poor alike, he 'recked not of the hatred of them all, for they needs must obey his will if they would have life, or lands or goods'. In creating the royal game preserve known as the New Forest in Hampshire, which still today encompasses over 90,000 acres, he demolished dwellings and entire villages. Nor was the New Forest the largest of the royal forests: the whole of Essex was subject to the forest laws; so were imm-

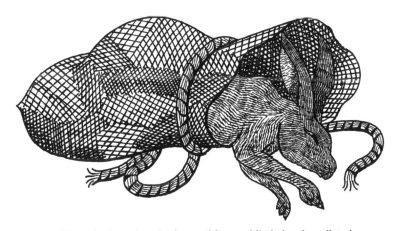

William I had poachers in the royal forests blinded and mutilated

57

ense tracts in the Midlands, around Windsor in Berkshire and in Oxfordshire where the hunting park of the Anglo-Saxon kings at Woodstock remained in royal hands until the beginning of the eighteenth century when Queen Anne gave it to the first Duke of Marlborough for the building of Blenheim Palace.

By the time of William I's grandsons, the royal forests had become so extensive that they may have covered almost a third of the country. A sizeable proportion of the rest of the land in England was enclosed as game preserves by the King's tenants-in-chief. Some of these preserves are still in private hands like Knowsley Park, the property of the eighteenth Earl of Derby. In others herds of red and fallow deer still roam between the rocks and bracken in the shade of ancient oak trees, as at Bradgate Park in Leicestershire where stags and does were once hunted by the medieval Earls of Winchester.

In August 1100, King William II was hunting in the New Forest when he was killed by an arrow, shot either accidentally or on purpose. His companions disappeared and his body, dripping blood, was taken by local serfs in a cart to Winchester where it was buried in the recently consecrated Cathedral whose tower soon afterwards collapsed, a disaster attributed to the unworthiness of the intolerable King for Christian burial.

'All things that are loathsome to God and to earnest men were customary in this land in his time,' wrote an English chronicler; 'and therefore he was loathsome to all his people, and abominable to God, as his end showed, forasmuch as he departed in the midst of his unrighteousness, without repentance and without expiation.'

His younger brother, Henry, who had also been hunting in the New Forest that day, immediately appropriated the royal treasure and insignia and had himself crowned in Westminster Abbey without delay. A severe man like his father, he was avaricious and crafty as well as cold-hearted; he had a passion for slaying deer and was said to have callously thrown a prisoner from a castle tower

The fierce forest laws amongst others earned William I widespread hatred

into the waters of a river far below. But he was anxious to persuade the English people that the lawless days of his brother's time were over. He imprisoned the detested Rannulf Flambard, the Bishop of Durham, William's deeply unpleasant chief adviser, in the Tower of London; he called Anselm back to Canterbury from France where he had been exiled by William; he issued a proclamation to the people promising to observe their rights; he put a stop to the depredations of the royal bodyguard who in his brother's day had become notorious for their robberies and rapes during the progresses of the royal household and its officials, the effective government of the country. He frequently went on progresses himself, visiting as many parts of his kingdom as he could and keeping a sharp eye upon the barons whose loyalty to the Crown was not to be taken for granted. 'Great awe there was of him,' recorded a chronicler, 'No man dared misdo another in his time.' Able to read and write – accomplishments then mastered by few, even of the highest rank – he acquired a reputation for scholarship as well as for firmness of hand: men called him Henry Beauclerk.

He won much goodwill by setting an example, soon to be followed by other Normans of high rank, by taking an English wife, Matilda, who was descended directly from Alfred the Great. Already the father of numerous children by a succession of mistresses, he had a son by Matilda, a boy of whom he held high hopes; and when this 'goodly heir' was drowned at sea with the entire crew and all but one of the passengers of the *White Ship*, the fastest vessel in his fleet, the King is said to have fallen unconscious to the ground at the woeful tidings and, as every English schoolboy used to know, he never smiled again.

The boy's mother had by then died herself. The King married again; but by his second wife, daughter of the Duke of Lower Lorraine, he had no children, and so he decided to make the drowned boy's sister, Matilda, his heir. This young woman was nineteen at the time of her brother's drowning. She had been married to the Holy Roman Emperor at the age of twelve and after his death had married Count Geoffrey of Anjou. Most of the barons did not take kindly to the thought of Matilda as their Queen. She had lived so long abroad that she seemed to them a foreigner; moreover they

**After the *White Ship* sank with his heir aboard,
Henry I is said to have never smiled again**

considered her far too autocratic and masterful for a woman.
Indeed, in the opinion of one observer, Annulf of Lisieux, she was
a woman who, apart from her undoubted beauty, had 'nothing of
the female in her'. Many barons preferred the claims of Matilda's
cousin, Stephen, Count of Blois – whose mother was William the
Conqueror's daughter – an affable, apparently easy-going and generous man who made many promises to his potential supporters,
offering them splendid rewards when he became King.

Stephen rushed over to England upon King Henry's death and
was welcomed into London where his brother, Henry of Blois,
the most powerful of the English bishops, persuaded the Archbishop of Canterbury to crown him at Westminster shortly before
Christmas 1135.

Outraged by her cousin's breach of faith, Matilda, who was
still in Normandy, appealed unsuccessfully to the Pope; then,
having done her best to make trouble for Stephen in England,

she landed in Sussex, travelled to Bristol where the barons of the West Country rallied to her support, and entered London in triumph. By then the English people, commoners and barons alike, had grown to resent Stephen's weak and erratic rule, the violence of his Flemish mercenaries, the power exercised by his influential Flemish adviser, William of Ypres, his scattering of the treasure which Henry I had accumulated, and his failure to abide by an oath to disafforest various royal lands. But Matilda was no better liked than Stephen. More arrogant and haughty than ever now that she was in control of the capital, she took the title of Queen without being crowned, appropriated lands to which she had no right, and when a deputation of the citizens of London petitioned for the observance of ancient laws she swore at them and drove them from the room. Soon afterwards she herself was driven out of London.

The years of quarrelling and fighting during which Stephen and Matilda and their baronial allies struggled against each other for the throne were so horrifyingly described by a monk of Peterborough – who lived in the midst of an area of peculiar turbulence – that they have been taken as characterizing the whole of the 'nineteen long winters' when 'God and his angels slept.' The barons 'greatly oppressed the wretched people by making them work at their castles,' the monk of Peterborough recorded, 'and when the castles were finished they filled them with devils and evil men. Then they took those whom they thought to have any goods, both men and women, and put them in prison for their gold and silver, and tortured them with pains unspeakable.'

Certainly there did occur such horrors. Geoffrey de Mandeville, grandson of one of William the Conqueror's knights, who changed sides as often as he conceived it in his interests to do so and wrung all manner of rights and privileges, including the earldom of Essex, from the opposing sides, rampaged about the country on indiscriminate raids, pillaging and burning, taking hostages and exacting blackmail. But Geoffrey de Mandeville was mortally

wounded by an arrow at Burwell in the summer of 1144; in 1147 recruitment for the Second Crusade drew many other adventurers out of the country; and at the beginning of the next year Matilda returned to Normandy, her cause lost. The worst troubles were then over. Stephen ruled for a further seven years until his death at Dover. Buried at the Cluniac Faversham Abbey, which he had founded, he was succeeded by the son of his rival Matilda and her second husband, who came to the throne as Henry II in 1154.

The feud between Stephen and Matilda drove years of turbulence

1154–1215
The House of
Plantagenet

t was claimed by one of the men about his constantly peripatetic court that the hands of Henry II, the first of the kings of the House of Plantagenet, were never empty: they always held either a bow or a book. He was certainly addicted to hunting, which he pursued with a ferocious energy. At the same time he had more learning than any European monarch of his time. From his earliest youth he had been 'imbued with letters and instructed in good manners beseeming a youth of his rank'; and, by the time he came to the throne as the age of twenty-one, his Latin was as fluent as his French. He was said, indeed, to have a good knowledge of all the tongues spoken between the Bay of Biscays and the Jordan, though evidently not of English. He never lost his love of literature nor his taste for intellectual discussion which he would carry on far into the night after a long day spent chasing deer. He never seemed tired, nor ever satisfied.

He transacted all his business standing up, pacing backwards and forwards on bowed legs covered with sores from the saddle, fiddling with his hunting gear, 'beguiling with scribbling or with whispered talk the enforced tranquility even of the hour of Mass'. He

Henry II hunted in the royal forests

was short and thickset with reddish hair cropped very short and a coarse complexion blotched with freckles. His eyes were prominent and often bloodshot and appeared to change colour when he flew into one of his alarming rages which were so uncontrollable that he would throw himself to the floor and grind the rushes that covered it between his teeth.

Yet 'all folk loved him', according to an English chronicler, 'for he did good justice and made peace.' Certainly, much could be forgiven a man who showed himself so determined to bring the disorders of King Stephen's reign to an end. Nineteenth-century historians were in the habit of giving Henry II more credit for his reforms than is his due; and it has since been emphasized how far the legal institutions of the country had already progressed before his coronation in 1154; yet his achievements were nevertheless remarkable, par-

ticularly so as England was but one part of his extensive dominions, which stretched from the Loire to the Pyrenees, and he had to spend much of his time on the Continent. In England he plunged into the tasks that faced him with almost demoniac energy, dismissing the Flemish mercenaries who had plagued his subjects for too long, demolishing scores of castles which had been built in Stephen's time, strengthening and widening the powers of his sheriffs – officials now trained in the law who were responsible for military as well as judicial affairs in their respective shires – recovering royal estates and aggrandizing royal influence at the expense of over-weening barons from whom he demanded money rather than military service, preferring to rely for armed support upon a militia composed of English freemen. As for the law, he encouraged the process, which had begun in the time of Henry I, whereby the jurisdiction of the king's courts and of the king's judges encroached upon that of the old courts whose hearings had been held in the hall of the local lord. There were large profits by way of fines and fees to be derived from jurisdiction, and the King was determined to reap them for himself. So cases which would formerly have been heard in the court of a local baron were now increasingly heard before royal itinerant justices who travelled about the country under guard, applying the law impartially at assizes and gradually establishing a common law in places of the customs of the manor which had previously varied not only from shire to shire but even from one community to another. Moreover, the jury system – whose origins can be traced to primitive trials in which witnesses were called forward to swear to the innocence of the accused – was at last replacing old English ordeals by fire and water and old Norman trials by battle.

Within the memory of men living in Henry II's time both these methods of determining guilt or innocence were still commonly practised. Indeed, trial by ordeal was not formally abolished until 1219. It took place in church, or in pits dug outside it, where fires were lit and bowls of water and bandages prepared. The witnesses, all of whom 'must be fasting and have abstained from their wives during the night', were sprinkled with holy water and given 'Gospels and the Symbols of Christ's Cross' to kiss. When the

Holding hot metal was one of the old English methods of trial by ordeal

water was boiling the accused's arm was bandaged and he was required to plunge it into the bowl to pick out a stone lying at the bottom. After three days the bandages were removed. Evidence of scalding was taken to be proof of guilt. As an alternative to the ordeal by water, the accused might be required to pick up a red-hot iron bar and hold it in his bare hand while he walked three paces. His hand was then sealed by the priest and if after three days a blister the size of a walnut had appeared he was declared guilty.

In trials by combat, which were still occasionally taking place in the fourteenth century, the contestants were attended by three priests who sang a Mass on the day of the trial and blessed the harness and weapons before the fight took place. Women and the old and infirm were excused from fighting personally and were allowed to appoint champions on their behalf. So were priests. Priests were also excused trial by ordeal and were required instead to eat a piece of bread and cheese before the altar. A prayer was made to God to send down the archangel Gabriel to stop the throat of the priest if he were guilty. If he managed to eat the food he was presumed innocent. The clergy had other privileges, too: when

accused of a crime they could be punished only in ecclesiastical courts and if found guilty there, while they might be unfrocked, they were more likely to be sentenced merely to suffer penances. In time this Benefit of Clergy came to be accepted as a plea against capital punishment in any court and could be claimed not only by priests and monks but by anyone accused of crime who could produce evidence that he was an educated man. The ability to read a few lines of a prescribed text – which illiterate prisoners often learned by heart with the help of accommodating gaolers – was taken as being sufficient evidence of education.

It was these exceptional privileges enjoyed by the clergy which brought King Henry into collision with the Church. His efforts to encourage a common law and to extend the scope of royal jurisdiction had not aroused much opposition from the barons, most of whom were happy enough to see the power of the more unpleasant of their number reduced for the sake of good order in the realm. But his attempts to have clergy who had been found guilty in ecclesiastical courts brought before civil courts for sentence, and to put a stop to appeals being made directly to Rome, angered the Church and led to his fateful quarrel with the Archbishop of Canterbury.

This Archbishop was Thomas Becket, son of a Norman merchant who had settled in London. A young man of exceptional gifts and striking personality, he had been appointed Chancellor of England, the King's chief secretary, before he was forty, the first man born in England to have held so high an office since the Conquest; and he had become so intimate a friend of the King that they were said to be inseparable. A year after Becket became Archbishop, a canon of Bedford was acquitted on a murder charge in the Bishop of Lincoln's court. The King demanded that the man should come forward to answer the charge in a civil court. Becket refused to allow this, countering with the demand that the King should come to plead his case in the ecclesiastical court at Canterbury. The dispute became more and more bitter until Becket thought it as well to go abroad. He spent six years on the Continent living an ascetic life – in marked contrast to the life he had formerly led at court and as the King's companion in the chase –

Thomas Becket was murdered in Canterbury Cathedral in 1170

threatening to excommunicate Henry and carrying out the threat against others whom he deemed to be enemies of the Church. Henry, who hated his former friend all the more because he had once loved him, retaliated by exiling all Becket's near relations and seizing his properties; and in 1170 he offered him a final insult, ignoring all precedents and defying the Pope, by getting the Archbishop of York to crown his eldest son as his partner in kingship. Fearing that he might have gone too far and that this defiance of the Church might provoke the Pope to prohibit Englishmen from participating in the sacraments, Henry allowed an agreement to be patched up and Becket returned to Canterbury. But soon fresh quarrels broke out; and Henry, while on a visit to his Continental possessions, was heard to burst out, 'What a parcel of fools and dastards have I nourished in my house that none of them will avenge me of this one upstart priest!' Four knights, taking the King at his word, and no doubt hoping for reward, sailed to England to murder the Archbishop. They came upon him in his cathedral and cut him down with their swords, the last blow splitting their victim's tonsured skull and spilling his brains on the stone floor of the north transept.

The body was buried next day in the crypt and almost immediately the grave became a place of pilgrimage, as it still was in and beyond Chaucer's time when, 'from every shires ende of Engelond', pilgrims wended their way to Canterbury, 'the holy blisful martir for to seke'. In 1173 the martyr was canonized and the following year the King thought it advisable to don pilgrim's weeds at Canterbury and do public penance for Becket's death, allowing himself to be scourged by all seventy monks of the chapter.

The remaining fifteen years of Henry's life were not happy ones. Soon after his marriage to Eleanor of Aquitaine, he had fallen in love with Rosamond, the daughter of Walter de Clifford, owner of extensive estates along the Welsh marches; and his attachment to this beautiful girl – that 'masterpiece of nature' whom her lover, so legend relates, sequestered from jealous eyes in a tower within a maze at Woodstock – was at least partly responsible for his unhappy relationship with his wife who, from her court at Poitiers, encouraged her sons in their opposition to him. For years Henry

Henry II's wife, Eleanor of Aquitaine, encouraged
their sons in their opposition to him

was intermittently at war with these sons and their ally, the King of France, until in 1189, having lost Le Mans and all the principal castles of Maine, he was forced to agree to a treaty with them and to pay an indemnity to the followers of the eldest surviving son, Richard. The sight of the name of Richard's younger brother, John, in lists of those who had fought against him, was more than the King could bear. Already dying, he turned his face to the wall and murmured, 'Enough! Now let things go as they may. I care no more for myself or for the world.'

He died on 6 July and two months later Richard was crowned at Westminster. Brave, dashing and impulsive, with a taste for poetry, he seemed more like a romantic cavalry leader than a king, and from the first was unwilling to devote his attention to the government of England where, in a reign that lasted almost ten years, he spent scarcely more than four months. He had been born at Oxford; but he spoke French and considered himself French, regarding England as a useful inheritance on which to raise money. At the time of his coronation he had already undertaken to take

Richard I joined the Third Crusade soon after his coronation in 1189

part in the Third Crusade, and he now instructed his agents to scour the country for funds to equip himself and his knights and fleet with appropriate power and splendour, 'offering for sale all he had,' so it was recorded, disposing of royal property left and right, selling his half-brother the archbishopric of York and releasing the King of Scotland from his allegiance for ten thousand marks. 'I would,' he is alleged to have declared, 'sell London itself if I could find a purchaser rich enough to buy it.' He died as no doubt he would have wished, in battle, killed by an arrow while besieging the castle of Chalus. In what was considered to be a characteristic gesture, he gave orders that the archer who had shot him should be spared; but, no less characteristically, the captain of his guard had the man flayed alive, and all his companions hanged, when the castle was captured.

John, who now succeeded to the English throne, bore no resemblance to his brother, either in character or in appearance,

although he was attractive when he chose to be, particularly to women for whom he had an appetite as keen as his father's. Scarcely more than five feet tall, he was good looking with widely-set eyes, long curly hair and a neatly trimmed beard. But of his character little that was favourable was ever said. One Victorian historian described him as 'a monster of iniquity', another as 'mean, false, vindictive, abominably cruel ... frivolous and slothful ... self-indulgent and scandalously immoral ... At once greedy and extravagant, he extorted money from his subjects and spent it in an ignoble manner. He had a violent temper and a stubborn disposition, but he lacked real firmness of mind, and was at heart a coward ... While he was abjectly superstitious, he was habitually profane and irreligious.' It had been his custom 'since the age of reason' to refuse Communion, and he thought nothing of interrupting a bishop's sermon to say he wanted his breakfast, loudly jangling the coins in his purse.

In recent years, efforts have been made to rescue the reputation of a man of whom it was suspected in his lifetime that he had not only murdered his nephew, son of his older brother, Geoffrey, who was the rightful heir to the throne, but had also hanged his wife's admirers from her bedposts.

It was true that John was an ingenious soldier; that, while extracting as much from England as his brother had done, he did not neglect the fleet; that he achieved a reputation amongst the ordinary people of England as a reasonable judge when indulging a taste for the processes of law by hearing cases in his own courts; that he was by no means a philistine, and had a well-chosen selection of books; that he was, for his time, remarkable for his personal cleanliness. But of his covetousness and callous insensitivity there can be no doubt. He treated churchmen with the coarse levity of William II, and extorted all he could by way of feudal dues from the barons while relentlessly pursuing their wives and demanding dowries from their daughters when they wished to marry. Neither lawyers nor merchants, nor knights nor burgesses escaped his depredations; and if the Jews were shielded from such attacks as they had suffered during the enthusiasm aroused by preparations for the Third Crusade, they were protected largely for the benefit of the royal treasury.

Like his father, he provoked a quarrel with the Pope by insisting upon the appointment as Archbishop of Canterbury of one of his advisers, John de Grey, Bishop of Norwich, 'a pleasant and facetious companion', and refusing to approve the consecration of the far more suitable Stephen Langton, a friend and fellow student of the Pope. By way of retaliation, the Pope placed England under an interdict, prohibiting the celebration of Mass; and in 1209 excommunicated the King who professed himself quite unconcerned by the punishment. Four years later, however, when England was threatened by a French invasion supported by the Pope, John was obliged to come to terms with the Papacy and to accept Langton as Archbishop.

It was a capitulation with fateful consequences, for Langton, an Englishman by birth, a cardinal and theological scholar of international repute, made no secret of his sympathy for the barons

in their differences with the King and, when certain magnates in the north and east broke out in revolt against royal tyranny and in defence of their customary rights, he acted as mediator and played a leading part in persuading the King that he must come to an agreement with the barons or face the consequences of civil war. Langton also helped to persuade the more extreme barons that they should include with their own demands certain others which might benefit the people as a whole.

The barons' charter, or Magna Carta as it came to be known, was presented by a delegation of their class to the King and his advisers in the early summer of 1215 at a conference at Runnymede, an island in the Thames four miles downstream from Windsor. After the negotiations of the day were over, John returned each evening to the Castle where he is reported to have rolled on the floor in his rage in the characteristic Angevin manner, clawing at the air, gnawing sticks and straw, his face mottled with blue spots. His violent protests were of no avail. In the end, with the utmost reluctance, he was obliged to put his seal to the Charter on 19 June.

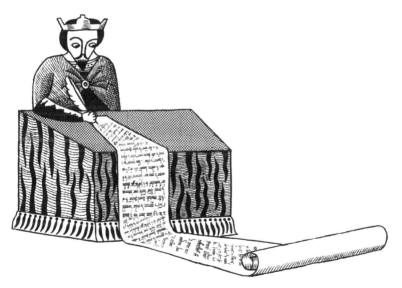

The Magna Carta was signed by King John on
Runnymede Island near Windsor in 1215

1215–1381
Crown and People

espite the importance subsequently attached to the Magna Carta both in Britain and the United States, the document was less the declaration of human rights it has often been supposed to be than a statement of the feudal and legal relationship between the Crown and the barons, a guarantee of the freedom of the Church and a limitation of the powers of the King. There are, however, clauses which promised more general rights. One in particular proclaimed that 'to none will we sell, to none will we refuse or delay right or justice'; another declared, 'No freeman shall be arrested or imprisoned ... or outlawed or exiled ... except by the lawful judgement of his peers and the laws of the land.' But virtually nothing was said about serfs.

Enraged by his having to sign the Charter, King John immediately denied its validity and, declaring that it had been wrung from him under duress, he prepared to fight the barons, while they, pretending to hold a tournament at Staines, assembled their own army and called upon the King of France to assist them. A French army landed in Kent and marched towards London; and John, ransacking castles and churches and burning crops on the way,

King John's treasures and loot were lost
when his army crossed the Wash

withdrew north-east into East Anglia. While his army was cross-
ing the neck of the Wash, the tide came in and all his treasures and
loot were lost. Distraught by this misfortune he went on discon-
solately to the abbey of Swineshead, which had been founded by
the Cistercians, an order of monks, an offshoot of the Benedictines,
one of the several monastic orders which had established abbeys in
England since the foundation of St Augustine's monastery at Canterbury towards the end of the sixth century. Here, after finishing
one of his habitually heavy meals with a surfeit of peaches and
sweet ale, John contracted dysentery, became feverish and died at
Newark on 19 October 1216 at the age of fifty.

His nine-year-old son and heir, who was taken to Gloucester to
be crowned as King Henry III, was then a tractable boy under the
tutelage of Hubert de Burgh, the chief justiciar or principal minister
in the kingdom, who fulfilled the duties which might roughly be
compared to those of a prime minister today. After successfully
defending Dover Castle, which he called 'the Key of England', from
the French army, Hubert de Burgh won a notable naval victory in
the Channel against a far greater number of French ships, whose
commander and crews were all slaughtered except for those from
whom ransoms might be extracted. Deprived by this defeat of his
expected reinforcements, the French King agreed to withdraw from
England upon the payment of a large sum of money, giving an undertaking, not fulfilled, to return Normandy to the English Crown.
After the withdrawal of the French, order was restored, Stephen

Langton, who had left the country in King John's reign, returned to Canterbury; and Hugh de Burgh administered the kingdom in the name of the young King.

As he grew up, however, Henry became more and more disinclined to take the advice of his English advisers, listening rather to his mother, Queen Isabella of Angoulême, to his wife, Eleanor, daughter of the Count of Provence, and to other foreign advisers in whose company he felt more at ease than he did with Englishmen. By the time of Hubert de Burgh's death in 1243, Henry was as much at odds with his barons as his father had been. He had grown into a shiftless and extravagant man, incompetent as a soldier and politician, and incapable of arousing respect or even much affection. He was extremely pious, attending Mass three times a day, taking great pleasure in religious ceremonies and lavishing money upon religious foundations, including Netley Abbey, overlooking Southampton Water, Westminster Abbey which was largely rebuilt in his reign, and the Domus Conversorum, a hostel for converted Jews, monuments from whose chapel are now in the Public Record Office which was built on its site.

For a time one of his particular favourites was Simon de Montfort, a Norman nobleman who had inherited the earldom of Leicester and had married the Queen's sister. Simon soon annoyed the King, however, by pressing for the same reforms as had been urged upon his father, and then exasperated him by presuming, although a Frenchman by birth, not only to become the acknowledged leader of the English barons – who were now meeting together more frequently than they had done in the past to discuss shared problems and affairs of state – but also to advocate the rights of less privileged classes. The King's demands for money to enable his son to be crowned King of Sicily and his brother to become King of the Romans brought matters to a head; and in 1258 it was demanded of Henry that he should appoint a new Great Council of twenty-four members, half of whom were to be nominated by the barons themselves. The members of this Council made their way with their armed retinues to Oxford where they called upon the King to rule with the advice of a smaller Council of fifteen nobles and bishops to be appointed by the recently created Great Council.

Henry III met Simon de Montfort while sheltering from the
rain on the steps of Durham House on the Thames

Encouraged by his wife and the Pope to defy the barons, Henry claimed that the Provisions of Oxford, which were a clear usurpation of royal power, had been forced upon him under duress. One day that summer, while the King was being rowed down the Thames in London, a storm broke out overhead, obliging him to seek shelter in Durham House, then occupied by Simon de Montfort who came out to greet him at the river steps and to assure him that the storm was over. 'I fear thunder and lightning exceedingly,' the King replied, 'but by God's head, I fear thee more than all the thunder and lightning in the world.'

He had good reason to do so; for when the inevitable civil war broke out between the King's supporters, mostly foreign mercenaries, and the baronial army led by Simon de Montfort, Henry was decisively beaten at Lewes in Sussex in May 1264, despite the routing on the left wing of the citizens of London by the King's son, Edward.

After this battle, while the King and Prince Edward were kept in prison, Simon de Montfort, Edward's godfather, summoned the Great Council to meet at Westminster together with representatives from every shire and nearly all the larger towns, a meeting which has been seen as that of the earliest parliament, a word not then in use in this sense, but one which later came to mean the supreme legislature of the country, comprising the sovereign, the Lords and the Commons assembled in Westminster.

The new constitution, however, was premature. Simon de Montfort's successes, his fiery temper and autocratic manner, the power he now wielded and the excesses of some of his adherents in their attacks upon royalists had made him many enemies. And when Prince Edward escaped from his captors, he was soon able to raise a formidable royal army far larger than that which Simon could bring against it. The two armies met at Evesham in August 1265. 'Let us commend our souls to God,' Simon declared when he saw the size of the enemy host, 'for our bodies are theirs.' So it proved to be. The resultant clash was a massacre rather than a battle; and Simon himself was hacked to pieces, the dismembered parts of his body being despatched for public display in towns which had supported him. Prince Edward, now twenty-six years old,

The royal army and the baronial army led by Simon
de Montfort met at Evesham in 1265

took over the administration of the realm from his father who had been wounded in the shoulder at Evesham, where, held as a hostage on the battlefield, he had not been recognized by his son's men.

Edward was a tall and commanding figure who ate sparingly and drank little but water. He was said to have been capable in his youth of acts of wanton cruelty, once helping his bodyguard to torture and mutilate a peasant whom they had come across on the road. But in recent years, while often merciless in dealing with defeated rebels, he had gained a reputation for courtesy and fair dealing, high intelligence and untiring energy. Devoted to his wife, he was deeply distressed when she died in Nottinghamshire and, having ordered that her body should be brought south to Westminster for burial, he asked that memorial crosses should be erected in all the towns in which the funeral cortege rested on the way. The last of these was put up in the small hamlet of Charing, now the busy London area of Charing Cross where a replica, based on drawings of the original cross – long since broken up for use as paving stones and knife handles – was placed in the railway station forecourt in 1865.

The Eleanor Cross at Charing Cross

Edward, who had taken the cross on the Eighth Crusade, was in Sicily when news reached him of his father's death in 1272; but since the realm was reportedly tranquil and in good hands, he made no haste in his journey home, sending couriers to England with his instructions and arriving himself at Dover on 2 August 1274.

Shrewd and painstaking, with an instinctive understanding of political possibilities, Edward presided over the continuing development of Parliament and the reform of the law, insisting upon the predominance of public over private jurisdiction, and making it clear that such baronial courts as still existed only did so by royal consent. He also became identified with the new spirit of aggressive nationalism, expelling from the country the Jews – who were already required to wear a distinguishing badge when walking the streets and forbidden to employ Christian servants – and marching at the head of armies intent upon the conquest of Wales and the subjugation of Scotland.

Northern and western Wales had long resisted penetration, the Celtic lords jealously retaining their old language and fostering amongst their people a profound dislike and distrust of English and Norman alike. The most gifted and powerful of these leaders, Llewelyn ap Gruffydd, who called himself Prince of Wales, maintained a long resistance to Edward's armies, but he was eventually killed in battle and Welsh independence was lost. To keep control over the Welsh people, a strong chain of castles was built, from Caerphilly Castle in the south to Beaumaris and Conway in the north and Harlech in the west. At one of the largest of these strongholds, Caernarfon Castle, Edward's heir was born and in 1301 created Prince of Wales, the title ever afterwards borne by the male heir to the English throne.

As Llewelyn's opposition had provided Edward with an excuse to subdue Wales, so the refusal of John de Baliol, who had recently become King of Scotland, to accept the overlordship of England gave him an excuse to march against the Scots. His army, thirty-five thousand strong, crossed the Tweed in March 1296 and, with the help of the long bow which Llewelyn's archers had used so effectively against them in Wales, defeated the Scots, took Baliol prisoner and forced him to surrender his crown. Edward returned in

triumph to England carrying with him the Stone of Scone on which the Kings of Scotland had long been crowned. He took it to Westminster Abbey where it was placed beneath the Coronation Chair which Edward had constructed to enclose it and which has been used for every coronation performed in the Abbey since his time.

The Scots, however, were not yet subdued. First under Sir William Wallace, who declared himself Guardian of Scotland, and was hanged, drawn and quartered after his defeat, then under Robert Bruce, who was crowned King of Scotland by the Bishop of St Andrews at Scone, resistance continued long after the death of Edward I who requested in his last hours that his bones should be carried from place to place wherever his army marched against the Scots so that he might, even in death, be said to have led it to victory. He asked also that beside his motto '*Pactum Serva*', 'Keep Faith', there should be inscribed on his tombstone the words '*Scotorum Malleus*', 'the Hammer of the Scots'. Edward's expensive campaigns necessitated his summoning his Council, now more generally known as Parliament, from time to time in order to raise money to pay for them, since the ordinary revenues of the Crown were insufficient for the waging of war and extraordinary taxation could not be levied without parliamentary approval. Concerned to have the votes of rich merchants and of the burgesses of the towns, he saw to it that they were represented at these meetings as well as nobles and prelates. At the Parliament of 1295 – later known as the Model Parliament because it was more representative than any of its predecessors – there were, for instance, among the earls and barons, the archbishops, bishops and heads of religious houses, two knights from each shire and two delegates from each city and borough. These men, representing the ordinary citizens of the towns, did not attend with any enthusiasm, knowing that their presence was required merely for financial reasons. Indeed, they had to be coerced by the threat of fines for non-attendance; but gradually they became more and more important as Parliament extended its control over taxation, and eventually sat separately from the nobles and upper clergy in their own chamber, the recently constructed Chapter House of Westminster

Robert Bruce

Abbey, before occupying the chamber that was especially built for them, the House of Commons, sometimes also now known as the Lower House, distinguishing it from the Upper House – the meeting place of the assembly of nobles which still includes bishops as well as peers – the House of Lords.

Despite unrest at home and costly wars abroad, the thirteenth century was, as a whole, a golden age for building. The Romanesque style had given way to the first phase of Gothic, a word which, as applied pejoratively to a supposedly barbarous architectural style, came into use in the seventeenth century. This first phase of Gothic became known as Early English, a style characterized by narrow lancet windows terminating in a pointed arch, by circular, or occasionally octagonal pillars and by moulded capitals, sometimes carved with foliage. It is seen at its most resplendent in Salisbury Cathedral, the west front of Wells Cathedral, the Angel Choir of Lincoln Cathedral – 'out and out,' in Ruskin's words, 'the

most precious piece of architecture in the British Isles' – and, more restrainedly, at York Minster where the stained glass is of an unsurpassed beauty.

Nor was it only an age of ecclesiastical building. At Oxford, where a university had been established around the church of St Mary the Virgin, three colleges, University, Balliol and Merton College, had been founded before the end of the thirteenth century and four more, Exeter, Oriel, Queen's and New College, were shortly to follow them. Here Robert Grosseteste, the great Bishop of Lincoln, in whose huge diocese Oxford then lay, was appointed Chancellor in about 1223; and Roger Bacon, the philosopher and one of the foremost experimental scientists of his time, had a study on a tower on Folly Bridge. At Cambridge, a university was also established, and St Peter's College or Peterhouse, the oldest of its colleges, was founded by the Bishop of Ely in 1281.

Law was not then taught at either Oxford or Cambridge, where the teaching was largely of grammar, philosophy and theology, the lectures being given in Latin, and this led to the establishment of hostels or inns for students of law in what are still the Inns of Court in London, namely Lincoln's Inn, Gray's Inn, the Middle Temple and the Inner Temple, the names of the last two Inns being derived from the Knights Templar, a brotherhood in arms devoted to the protection of pilgrims in the Holy Land. Their church here, Temple Church, is a fine example of the Transitional style between Romanesque and Early English, a style which can also be seen in the nave of Fountains Abbey and the retrochoir of Chichester Cathedral.

While the masons were at work at Chichester, Edward I's son and heir, Edward II, was crowned at Westminster. Ill-educated and indiscreet, Edward II affected the manners of the grooms of his stables whose company he preferred to that of his father's ministers, most of whom he dismissed from office. An excessively heavy drinker, he had a petulant temper and would often strike across the face members of his household who offended him. He was frequently to be found engaged in amateur theatricals when affairs of state awaited his attention or in the company of his intimate friend and presumed lover, Piers Gaveston, the grasping, insolent son of a Gascon knight whom his father had banished but

whom he now recalled and created Earl of Cornwall to the fury of the English barons. The barons were not, however, prepared to tolerate Gaveston for long: in 1312 a group of them carried him away a prisoner and cut his head off.

The problem of Scotland could not be settled so expeditiously. Robert Bruce was still at large in command of a formidable army north of the border, capturing one by one the castles still in English hands; and when a large English army, at least three times the size of his own, marched against him he skilfully outmanoeuvred it, trapped it in a bog beside the Bannock Burn on 24 June 1314 and overwhelmed it, sending King Edward, who had remained at the rear with attendant bishops, flying for his life to Dunbar and driving his surviving soldiers after him.

More despised than ever, Edward returned to England where he solaced himself with his new favourites, the Despensers, father and son, men as avaricious and grasping as Gaveston had ever been. The history of the rest of Edward's reign is a tale of blood and betrayal. The barons rose up against the King and the Despensers and were defeated in 1322 at Boroughbridge in Yorkshire where the leader of the baronial party, the Earl of Lancaster, was taken prisoner and later beheaded; Edward's wife left him and took their son to France where the rebel exile, Roger Mortimer, eighth Baron of Wigmore and owner of large estates on the Welsh marches, became her lover. He and the Queen returned to England in 1326 with a force of mercenaries, soon to be joined by numbers of English supporters of all classes as anxious to see an end to Edward's rule as were the Queen and Mortimer. They defeated the King's forces and forced him to abdicate in favour of his son, now fourteen years old. Both Despensers were forced to suffer a traitor's death; and Edward was imprisoned in Berkeley Castle north of Bristol. Held in a dark cell over a charnel-house, it was hoped he would contract some fatal disease; but surviving this treatment he was murdered, traditionally by having a red-hot spit thrust up his anus into his entrails, an end, so it was said, befitting so shameless a sodomite. His apparently unharmed body, displayed for a time as evidence of his death from natural causes, was taken for burial to the Abbey of St Peter, now Gloucester Cathedral, where the effigy upon his tomb

beneath a finely carved and many-pinnacled canopy is one of the most beautiful alabaster figures made in the fourteenth century.

The King's son who ordered the making of this tomb and came to the throne as Edward III in 1327 seemed to be in many ways the very antithesis of his father. Like him he was extravagant, ostentatious and intemperate; but, whereas the father was craven, the son was extravagantly brave; and, while Edward II had been an actor *manqué*, Edward III thought of himself as an Arthurian knight, living in a lost world of romantic chivalry. After a brief foray into Scotland, he turned his attention to France, partly to provide exciting and profitable adventures for those who might otherwise make trouble at home, partly because the Scots were turning increasingly to France for help against the English, and partly to thwart French moves against the cities of Flanders with which the by now extremely prosperous English wool trade was so closely connected. Claiming the French throne through his mother, Isabella, daughter of Philip IV, he declared a war that was to last for a hundred years. At first he was brilliantly successful: he won a great naval victory at Sluys on 24 June 1340, then an equally decisive land battle near Calais at Crécy where his sixteen-year-old son, soon to be known as the Black Prince because of his unusually dark armour, greatly distinguished himself and, so it is said, by adopting as his own the crest of three feathers and the maxim '*Ich dien*' ('I serve') of the blind King of Bohemia, who had been slain in the opposing army, provided a badge and motto for all future Princes of Wales.

The King went on to take Calais; and in 1356 at Poitiers his son, the Black Prince, won another victory over the French King who was taken prisoner and held to ransom. By the Treaty of Bretigny, Edward III gained much of what he had fought for, absolute control over great territories in the south-west that stretched almost from the Loire to the Pyrenees and, in the north, Calais and Ponthieu.

After his earlier victories Edward III had returned home in triumph with wagonloads of plunder, clothes and furs, feather beds and the spoils of foreign cities. It was said that 'all England was filled with the spoils of the King's expedition, so that there was not a woman who did not wear some ornament, or have in her house fine linen or some goblet, part of the booty' brought home.

The Star, part of the regalia
of the Order of the Garter

Yet the wild extravagance of the victors' celebrations seemed
to some chroniclers wickedly wanton, in particular the merriment
at Windsor whence there came reports of the most prodigal festivities, of 'feasts complete with richness of fare, variety of dishes,
and overflowing abundance of drinks'. In the Upper Ward of the
Castle, the King ordered the construction of a magnificent circular
stone feasting hall in which would be held the meetings of the
knights of a new 'Round Table in the same manner and conditions
as the Lord Arthur, formerly King of England, appointed it'. These
knights were to be bound together by 'a badge of unity and
concord', a garter. The story went – and recent research has ind-
icated that it may well be true – that the King was dancing at a ball
in the Castle with Joan, Countess of Salisbury, when her garter fell
off. Edward stooped and picked it up. Some of the other dancers
saw him do so and began to tease him. He replied sharply, speaking
in French which was the language he used in ordinary conversation
– though he is believed to be the first King of England after the

Conquest, with the possible exception of Henry I, to have been able to speak English – '*Honi soit qui mal y pense*' ('shame on him who thinks ill of it'), thus providing the motto of the oldest extant order of knighthood in Europe.

This was in 1348, a year in which the festivities at Windsor seemed all the more reprehensible to the chroniclers, for it was the dreadful year in which 'the cruel pestilence, terrible to all future ages, came from parts over the sea to the south coast of England, into a port called Melcombe in Dorsetshire'. This plague or Great Mortality, much later to be known as the Black Death, 'passed most rapidly from place to place,' recorded the Registrar of the Court of Canterbury, 'swiftly killing ere mid-day many who in the morning had been well, and without respect of persons'. The first symptoms were swellings in various parts of the body, particularly in

The Black Death spread rapidly across the country, leaving some towns and villages entirely wiped out

the groin and under the arms, then the eruption of black pustules. Delirium soon followed, and the vomiting of blood. Few who were infected escaped death, and that within a few hours. When the summer of 1348 gave way to colder weather the spread of the plague was halted for a time but when spring came it renewed its course more virulently than ever. The towns were the worst affected places; but small villages did not escape and in some the inhabitants were entirely wiped out. Only the remote areas of the north-west, the mountainous regions of Wales and Scotland and west Cornwall, remained immune.

It has been estimated that almost half the people in the country perished. It does, indeed, seem likely that the population, which had risen to about 4,250,000 by 1300, had fallen to about 2,500,000 by 1380. The Black Death was not entirely responsible for this

sharp fall: there were other outbreaks of plague and occasional famine, while sheep farming, which required a relatively small labour force, was extending over large areas at the expense of corn growing. But the Black Death, a fearful visitation which contributed much to the macabre nature of later medieval literature, was undoubtedly the main cause of the dramatic fall in population and of the acceleration of far-reaching changes already noticeable in English society.

The sharp decline in the population of England naturally resulted in an acute labour shortage as well as a plentiful supply of land for the surviving peasants. Many peasants were able to increase their holdings by taking over the fields of those who had died; others, who had no land, were able to demand greater rewards for their services and went off to other manors if they did not get them. The King, preoccupied with his foreign wars and, in his premature senility, with his rapacious mistress, Alice Perrers, allowed the government to fall into the hands of his fourth son, John of Gaunt, Duke of Lancaster, who was thought to be intent on gaining a controlling influence over the King's grandson, later Richard II, or even to be contriving to gain the crown for himself. In an effort to overcome their financial and social problems the government in 1351 issued a Statute of Labourers which made it a crime for peasants to ask for more wages or for their employers to pay more than the rates laid down by the Justices of the Peace, the local gentry with judicial powers to try cases relating to public order in the counties, the ancestors of the present Justices who still have power to try lesser cases, committing the more serious to a higher court. A later Statute proposed that any labourer who left his place of work to seek higher wages should be branded with the letter 'F' on his forehead as a sign of falsehood. It soon even became a crime for a labourer to dress as though he were a landlord and for 'common lewd women' to dress like 'good noble dames'.

Such repressive measures, combined with the imposition of a series of taxes known as poll taxes and levied on everyone over fifteen, caused deep and widespread discontent which was exacerbated by resentment against the riches and corruption of the higher clergy. John Wyclif, for a time Master of Balliol College,

Oxford, spoke for thousands when he urged the disendowment of the Church and a return to evangelical poverty; and his 'poor priests', known as Lollards – a word meaning mumbler of prayers applied to them derisively by William Courtenay, Archbishop of Canterbury – went about the country preaching Wyclif's doctrines and condemning the ecclesiastical hierarchy and the material possessions of the Church. Speaking more bluntly and, on occasions, crudely, John Ball, an eloquent and fiery excommunicated priest, marched from market place to churchyard, castigating the ways of the clergy and preaching upon the contentious text:

When Adam dalf [dug] and Eve span
Who was thanne a gentilman?

Soon whole districts were in uproar. Manors and religious houses were attacked; lords and priors murdered; and the cry went up, 'Death to all lawyers. John Ball hath rungeth your bell!'

Led by one Walter, a man supposed to have been either an ex-soldier or a highwayman but generally known as Wat Tyler because of his trade, the men of Kent and Essex, forming bands of armed villagers and townsmen, descended on London in June 1381, releasing John Ball from Maidstone gaol on the way. They poured into Southwark; ransacked Lambeth Palace, the Archbishop of Canterbury's house since the end of the twelfth century; crossed London Bridge between the houses which had been built on it from bank to bank; marched down Fleet Street; burst into the Temple where they burned the lawyers' rolls; opened the gates of the Fleet prison; attacked the houses of foreign merchants; and, 'like packs of hungry wolves', made their way to Savoy Palace, the great mansion in the Strand which had been granted by Henry III to his wife's uncle, the Count of Savoy, and was now occupied by the King's hated uncle, John of Gaunt.

The Duke escaped but his doctor and sergeant-at-arms were both killed; the palace was ransacked and set alight; the explosion of a box of gunpowder consigned to the flames brought down the Great Hall; and thirty-two men who were drinking the Duke's wine were trapped when the cellar ceiling collapsed on them.

Wat Tyler led the Peasants' Revolt of 1381 during which the
Lord Treasurer and the Archbishop of Canterbury were beheaded
on Tower Hill and their heads paraded on spikes

The mob, 'howling like men possessed', now turned their attention to the Tower. Forcing their way across the drawbridges and through the gates, they dashed through the Great Hall and the Wardrobe into the private apartments of the King's mother where they tore down her hangings and cut her bedclothes into ribbons. She herself escaped in the confusion; but, in the Chapel of St John, the rebels came upon the Lord Treasurer and the Archbishop of Canterbury praying before the altar. They dragged them out and, with other victims, beheaded them on Tower Hill, parading their heads about the city on spikes. Meanwhile, another rebel leader, Jack Straw, led his men north to attack the Treasurer's house at Highbury and to burn down the Priory of St John, Clerkenwell.

The next day, 15 June, the fourteen-year-old King Richard met the rebels at Smithfield in an open field where horse sales were held, and there he acceded to most of their requests. Yet Tyler's arrogant disrespect so enraged the Lord Mayor, William Walworth, a fishmonger, that he lashed out at the man with the flat of his sword, knocking him off his horse to the ground where he was stabbed to death with a dagger which is displayed, with various treasures of the Fishmongers' Company, in Fishmongers' Hall, King William Street. Brandishing their weapons, the rebels advanced upon the King's retinue. But Richard rode towards them, calling out, 'Sirs, will you kill your King? I am your captain. Follow me.' Responding to this plea, they rode away with him towards Clerkenwell where they dispersed, trusting him to keep the promises he had made to them. But these were all broken on the grounds that they had been obtained under duress; and, when reminded of his undertakings to abolish feudal services, the King is said to have riposted, 'Villeins you are, and villeins you will remain.' Although the poll tax was abandoned, the survivors of the revolt returned to their homes to resume their seemingly immutable lives.

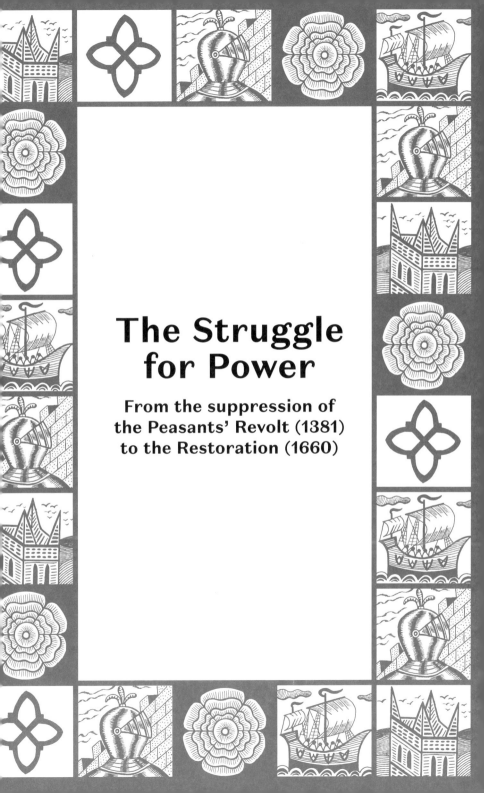

The Struggle for Power

**From the suppression of
the Peasants' Revolt (1381)
to the Restoration (1660)**

1381–1485
Twilight of the
Middle Ages

lthough the wearisome daily round of a farm labourer changed little during the fourteenth century,
society was slowly being transformed nevertheless, and there was beginning to be discerned a
gradual shift in the balance of power. Not only were
industrious peasants increasing their holdings in the aftermath
of the Black Death; not only were those who had no holdings
successfully pressing for higher rewards for their labour; but landlords were being obliged by the labour shortage to let land either
for money rent or for payment in kind, while many of their tenants
were becoming quite prosperous yeomen farmers whose interests were more closely identified with those of the lesser gentry
than with those of landless labourers. The Pastons, for example, the
well-to-do Norfolk family whose correspondence provides so illu-
minating a picture of late medieval domestic life, had but lately risen
from the lowly estate of husbandmen bound to the land for life.

The landscape in which these people spent their lives had been
changing for some time, too. The years immediately before the
Black Death had been an era of economic decline: large areas of
land had fallen out of agricultural use; water had poured back over

acre upon acre of drained fenland; and the foundation of new towns came almost to an end. The Black Death had much accelerated this depression and it was to be many years before the process was reversed. Indeed, the decline in arable farming continued long into the next century as the demand for wool and its price increased and ship after ship sailed with exports to the Continent. To create more land for sheep, arable fields were made into pasture; and whole villages were destroyed and their inhabitants evicted to make way for new flocks. At the same time the fortunes being made by wool farmers and wool merchants were being used to create the buildings which are still so distinctive a feature of the English scene. In nearly every English county, by wealthy tinners in Devon and Cornwall, as well as by individuals and communities doing so well in the wool trade, churches were being built and reconstructed in the style known as Perpendicular, the last stage of Gothic, a style distinguished by large windows with a predominance of vertical lines in their stone tracery and regular horizontal divisions, and by the kind of fan vaulting to be seen in the cloisters of Gloucester Cathedral. Beautiful examples of Perpendicular churches can be seen, for example, in Wiltshire at Steeple Aston, in Somerset at Huish Episcopi, in Norfolk at Salle, in Gloucestershire at Cirencester; in Suffolk at Long Melford as well as at Lavenham where, indeed, the whole town is a monument to the prosperity of the wool and clothing trade of the late Middle Ages.

In Kent, too, and in the north-west Midlands are numerous examples of the comfortable houses being built by merchants and yeomen farmers whose wealth, if not power, was beginning to rival that of the old ruling class. Castles were still being built as well as houses, several of them brick like Tattershall Castle in Lincolnshire and Herstmonceux in Sussex; and these, with more doors and many more windows, were becoming – while still formidable enough in appearance – more like homes than fortresses, since the increasing use of gunpowder and the power of cannon had rendered the most sturdy defences vulnerable to assault.

Bricks were not a new building material. Imported from the Continent and known as Flanders tiles, they had been used since the beginning of the thirteenth century when Little Wenham Hall

Bricks and half-timbered architecture became popular in the Middle Ages

had been built on the borders of Suffolk and Essex. This, however, was an unusual example until the brick buildings of France attracted the attention of knights fighting there. The English word 'brick' from the French '*brique*' did not even enter the language until 1416; and the town wall at Kingston Upon Hull, built in the second half of the fourteenth century of locally-made bricks, was probably the first major public work to be constructed in England of this material. Thereafter brick became much more commonly used even in districts where the local material was stone, as at Compton Wynyates in Warwickshire. Two and a half million bricks were used in the building of Eton College in the ten years after its foundation in 1440.

The heyday of brick had not yet come, however. Most houses were still made of timber or stone. So were most late medieval bridges, several of which still survive, notable examples in stone being those over the Camel at Wadebridge in Cornwall and over the Thames at Abingdon in Oxfordshire. Also, of course, of stone were the finest masterpieces of the Perpendicular style, such as the West Front of Beverley Minster, Eton College Chapel and the

Chapel of St George at Windsor, which was dedicated to the obscure third- or fourth-century martyr who, for reasons unexplained, had become England's patron saint. This chapel was begun in 1478 by Edward IV, determined to outdo Eton College Chapel, the nearby foundation of his rival and victim, Henry VI.

Henry VI's grandfather, the eldest surviving son of John of Gaunt, Duke of Lancaster, and known as Henry Bolingbroke after the Lincolnshire Castle where he was born, had supplanted his cousin, Richard II, in 1399 and had become the first of the Lancastrian kings. In Westminster Hall – the splendid Norman banqueting hall built by William II which is the only surviving part of the original Palace of Westminster – Henry had called out in English, long since the language not only of ordinary people but also of the law courts, 'In the name of Fadir Son and Holy Ghost, I Henry of Lancaster chalenge this Rewme of Ingland and the Corone.' The Archbishops of York and Canterbury had led him to the throne vacated by the deposed Richard II and, soon afterwards, he had been anointed with the oil which the Virgin Mary had miraculously given to St Thomas in his exile.

Yet while accepted by Parliament, Henry IV was no more able to come to satisfactory terms with its members than his predecessor had been. Beset by financial and administrative problems, by conspirators in his own country and by rebels in Wales, he fell ill in 1412 with what the chroniclers described as leprosy but may well have been syphilis with which leprosy was then often confused. He died in the Jerusalem Chamber at Westminster Abbey, where he had been praying before St Edward's shrine, and was buried in Canterbury Cathedral, where his magnificent tomb lies behind the high altar.

His son, Henry V, who was crowned in a violent snowstorm in April 1413, was every inch a soldier. The back of his neck and the sides of his head were shaved, as the heads of soldiers were, so that his hair, thick, brown and uncurled, looked like a round fur cap. He was considered a handsome man, though the long and prominent nose, the thin eyebrows, the high smooth brow, the very red and tightly compressed lips and the heavy lantern jaw are features no longer admired. His energy was legendary and men looking at him

found grounds for hope that his father's reign, which had opened with usurpation, rebellion, plague and persecution and had ended in fear, lassitude and gloom, would be followed by a new age, as brilliant and adventurous as that of the young King's great-grandfather, Edward III.

Henry was certainly as anxious to fulfil that dream as he was to engage in some foreign adventure which would distract the attention of his enemies from problems at home and from his far from indisputable title to the English throne. Reviving the claims of his ancestors, he required the return of territories that had been granted to Edward III by the Treaty of Bretigny and later demanded the French crown by right of succession from his great-great-grandmother, Isabella, daughter of Philip IV. And at Agincourt on St Crispin's Day 1415, in an astonishing pitched battle which lasted barely three hours, his depleted, exhausted and hungry army routed a French force four or five times its size, losing no more than a hundred men to the enemy's seven to ten thousand dead. After this extraordinary victory, Henry was able to impose humiliating terms upon the French King whose daughter he married and whose heir he became. The leadership of all Christendom was now within his grasp and his thoughts turned to a new crusade against the Infidel. But his health broke down in the summer of 1422 and at the age of thirty-five he died at Vincennes. His body was embalmed and brought home to England to be interred in Westminster Abbey in a resplendent tomb beneath the Chantry of Henry V.

He left England in the care of a regent and a baby king who eventually, having neither his powers of leadership nor his degree of parliamentary support and having to contend with the rising force of French national pride and its inspired epitome, Joan of Arc, was to lose all that his father had fought for by the time the Hundred Years' War ended in 1453.

Henry VI, who was only eight months old at the time of his accession, was to lose more than France. A kind, simpleminded man more interested in his religious observances and benefactions than in government, he lost his reason in 1453 and his life in 1471 when, a prisoner in the Tower, he was found dead in his cell, having passed away, so it was announced, out of 'pure displeasure and melancholy'.

Henry V was crowned in 1413
Overleaf: The English army of Henry V met
the French at Agincourt, 1415

During the last years of his unhappy reign, his supporters had
been fighting other claimants to the throne in the dynastic conflict
known as the Wars of the Roses. The Lancastrians – represented by
Henry VI and led by Henry's Queen Margaret and the descendants
of John of Gaunt by his mistress, later wife, Catherine Swynford –
were the faction of the red rose, one of the several emblems of their
house. Their opponents, the Yorkists – led by Richard, Duke of York,
a descendant of Edward III, and by Richard Neville, Earl of Warwick,
the most powerful noble in the realm, known as 'The Kingmaker'
– bore the white rose. Intermittently, for thirty years, these two
factions quarreled and fought, causing havoc in the areas where
they clashed, yet, when their armies had passed by, leaving the
merchants and the great mass of the people to carry on with their
work as in times of perfect tranquillity. At length the Duke of York's

son, Edward, emerged the victor, after deposing King Henry VI in 1461 and inflicting a series of defeats on the Lancastrians, culminating in their rout in 1471 at Tewkesbury.

With nearly all his leading opponents either killed in the battle or executed afterwards, Edward's position was now secure; and as King Edward IV he set about restoring the finances of the Crown and the disrupted export trade of the country. Virtually dispensing with Parliament, so many of whose members had been killed in the recent wars, he raised money by all the other means open to him, taking care to ensure that all the revenues to which the Crown was entitled were collected and administered with the utmost efficiency.

Grateful to him for restoring order to the country and helping to give it a large measure of prosperity, the citizens of London regarded Edward as 'the most noble of kings'. So did their wives, one of whom, Jane Shore, whose husband was a Lombard Street goldsmith, became the most celebrated of Edward's countless mistresses, giving her name to some of London's most squalid eighteenth-century brothels. Over six foot three inches tall, handsome, autocratic and wonderfully energetic, Edward IV was a man

The dynastic battle between the Lancastrians and the
Yorkists was known as the War of the Roses

**Jane Shore was the most celebrated
of Edward IV's mistresses**

of insinuating charm and friendly bonhomie. His subjects were prepared to forgive him much; and it was not until the end of his life that his debaucheries and increasingly unscrupulous conduct turned them against him.

He died in 1483 and his thirteen-year-old son was proclaimed his successor as Edward V. While awaiting his coronation the new King and his younger brother were lodged in the Tower; and it was announced that for the time being their uncle, Edward IV's brother, Richard, Duke of Gloucester, had been appointed to the office of Protector.

To some historians, Richard of Gloucester remains the monster that William Shakespeare portrayed. To others, discrediting the propaganda of those who defeated him, he is a paragon. Undoubtedly he was not the sanguinary hunchback of popular imagination;

nor was he guilty of many of the atrocious crimes attributed to him. Yet he was not a man whose character was out of tune with the ruthless spirit of his times; and, although there is no reliable evidence that he was responsible for the murders of Edward V and his brother, who never emerged from the Tower, there is also no evidence that he was not.

Whether responsible for the crime or not, he did not live to profit from it long. For on 22 August 1485 at Bosworth Field in Leicestershire, in the last battle of the Wars of the Roses, he lost his crown and his life to yet another claimant to the throne, Henry Tudor, the son of a Welsh knight, whose mother was a great-granddaughter of John of Gaunt. Soon after his victory, Henry Tudor married Edward IV's daughter, Elizabeth, thus uniting the Houses of Lancaster and York, a reconciliation symbolized by the red and white rose of the House of Tudor.

The fifteenth century was now drawing to a close. It was a century described by the Victorian historian, Bishop William Stubbs, as 'futile, bloody and immoral' and by a historian of our own day as the background to a society 'violent, dirty and overdressed'. But it was also the age of John Lydgate's *Troy Book* and of Sir Thomas Malory's *Le Morte d'Arthur*; of Reginald Ely, the Norfolk mason, who built the first court of Queen's College, Cambridge as well as the Chapel of King's College; of Henry Chichele, the Archbishop of Canterbury, who founded All Souls College, Oxford; and of John Glasier who provided the College with some of its beautiful painted glass; of the carvers of William of Wykeham's Chantry in Winchester Cathedral and of the monument in St Albans Cathedral to Henry V's brother, Humfrey, Duke of Gloucester, who presented his large collection of manuscripts to the Bodleian Library, Oxford, where the splendid room in which they were housed still bears his name.

Richard III, the last of the Plantagenet Kings,
was killed at Bosworth Field, 1485

1485–1603
Tudor England

ccording to a tradition preserved by Shakespeare, when Henry Tudor was brought to London as a boy to be presented to Henry VI, the King, struck by the intelligence of his looks, declared, 'Lo, surely, this is he to whom both we and our adversaries shall hereafter give place.' Several portraits of Henry VII, as well as the bust of him by Petro Torrigiani, now in the Victoria and Albert Museum, do, indeed, present the impression of a remarkable man, astute and wary, calculating but not without mercy, grave yet responsive to humour. He was clearly a ruler as capable as any of restoring order to a stricken country, of bringing solvency and honour to the Crown, and of continuing the work begun by his Plantagenet and Lancastrian predecessors. He chose his servants well, esteeming capacity above high birth, ensuring that his financial and judicial agents lost no opportunity of gathering in every penny due to the King who personally supervised their accounts, straining to obtain all that could be gleaned from royal lands and the administration of royal justice, allowing the commissioners of his minister, Richard Foxe, Bishop of Winchester, and of his Lord Chancellor, John Morton, Archbishop of Canterbury,

to raise money by the method which became known as Morton's Fork, a form of assessment that extracted money both from those who lived frugally, on the grounds that they must have savings, and from those who lived in grand style, on the grounds that they must be rich. Morton, Foxe and the King's other principal advisers, about half of them bishops, were members of his Privy Council, now effectively the government of the country, the Great Council being in process of development into the House of Lords.

The Lords had been much weakened and reduced by the recent wars – several noble families having been completely wiped out and not replaced by the creation of new peerages – while the Commons – comprising for the most part knights elected by their shires and burgesses from the towns – were summoned only when their assent was needed for the passing of new laws or the raising of taxes. The Privy Council was, therefore, under the King supreme; and its powerful judicial body, the Court of Star Chamber – so known because of the decoration of the ceiling in the room where it met in Whitehall Palace – made its rulings unhampered by the Common Law which was administered by the unpaid Justices of Peace in the country at large. The Council of the North was held responsible for the administration of the northern counties – in so far as these still largely wild regions could be said to be susceptible to royal rule at all – but, in matters of concern to the nation as a whole, the Privy Council had to be consulted.

The accession of the Tudor dynasty in 1485 did not, of course, immediately put an end to strife and rebellion. The impostor, Lambert Simnel, the son of a pastry cook, claiming to be the nephew of Edward IV and crowned in Dublin as King Edward VI, mustered sufficient support for an invasion of England in 1487; but he was soon defeated, and his survival as a scullion in the royal kitchens, and later as a falconer, shows how confident of his safety the King had already become in a country weary of conflict and only too ready to accept autocracy for the sake of peace. Another impostor, Perkin Warbeck, claiming to be the younger of the two princes held in the Tower in the reign of Richard III, also invaded England; but he, too, was soon forced to submit to the King's troops.

Nor did the accession of the Tudors and the ending of the Wars

William Caxton, the first English printer

of the Roses bring the Middle Ages to a convenient close. Most people in the country, living and working in their age-old ways, were unaware that any notable change had taken place. A Statute of the second year of the King's reign which referred to him as 'the Sovereign Lord of this land for the time being' might well have seemed well phrased to them, had they ever heard of it. Yet profound changes were, nevertheless, taking place. The ideas of the Renaissance, that flowering of art, literature and politics under the influence of Greek and Roman models, which had begun in northern Italy in the previous century or earlier, was now spreading across Europe and inducing men and women to regard themselves and their lives in relation to the world in which they lived rather than to the superhuman world of the old-fashioned theologians and schoolmen. This was the age of John Colet, Dean of St Paul's Cathedral and founder of St Paul's School, who returned to England from Italy in 1496, and of Desiderius Erasmus who came to Oxford from Paris two years later, as well as of William Caxton whose press at Westminster was busily printing the books which were to disseminate the new ideas of their time.

Also, the world was expanding: Portuguese explorers were voyaging ever further south down the coast of Africa; and in 1497 Vasco da Gama made his momentous journey round the Cape of

Good Hope to India. Five years earlier, the Genoese, Christopher Columbus, having failed to persuade the English and Portuguese kings to invest in his enterprise, had sailed across the Atlantic and planted the Spanish flag upon the shores of the New World, claiming it for his sponsors, Ferdinand and Isabella of Spain.

For centuries England had been regarded as an offshore island of relatively small concern in the affairs of western Europe. She was now becoming a nation and a market of importance not only to the Low Countries and the states of the Baltic but also to France and Spain. She was being recognized as a country of expert seamen and experienced merchants, a country whose resources, as yet scarcely known, would one day make her powerful, a country occupying a position which might have been especially designed to enable her to take advantage of the opportunities of trade which the discoveries of the century's explorers now offered Europe. While the marriage of Henry VII's daughter, Margaret, to King James IV of Scotland might have been seen merely as a prudent means of keeping the peace by the union of dynasties – like Henry's own marriage to Elizabeth of York – the match between Henry's son, Prince Arthur, and Catherine of Aragon, daughter of the Spanish King Ferdinand, could not but be interpreted as a sign of England's rising reputation in the eyes of the world.

When Henry VII died in 1509 at fifty-two, an age greater than that reached by any of his four immediate predecessors, he left his son and heir an immense fortune, even though he had not denied himself the pleasures of building. He had lavished immense sums of money upon Henry VII's Chapel in Westminster Abbey – a superb example of the late Perpendicular or Tudor Gothic style – had contributed towards the cost of several institutions established by his mother, Lady Margaret Beaufort, foundress of St John's College and Christ's College, Cambridge, and had spent enormous sums upon the navy whose flagship, the *Mary Rose*, which sank off Portsmouth in 1545, was recently raised and can now be seen in the naval base at Portsmouth.

The King's eldest son, Prince Arthur, fourteen years old at the time of his marriage to Catherine of Aragon, had died at Ludlow Castle soon after the wedding. He boasted coarsely that he had

been 'six miles into Spain'; but his bride maintained that she was still a virgin at his death. The Pope was accordingly persuaded to grant a dispensation so that she could marry his younger brother, Henry, who had by then become King of England.

Henry VIII was an attractive young man of high intelligence, numerous accomplishments and boundless self-confidence, enjoying to the full both the sports and pastimes of the royal parks and palaces and the intellectual pleasures of a court which was graced, or soon to be graced, by Sir Thomas More, the humanist scholar and statesman and author of *Utopia*, the poets Skelton, Surrey and Wyatt, and the painter Hans Holbein whose portraits and whose followers' portraits of the magnificent King were to adorn the country houses of numerous of his awed and faithful subjects.

The King pursued his pleasures and interests with a seemingly tireless energy; but to work he brought little of the application of his father, content to leave much of the Crown's business in the highly capable and grasping hands of Thomas Wolsey. The son of an Ipswich butcher, Wolsey was immensely rich and powerful, a Cardinal, Archbishop of York as well as Lord Chancellor. His portly figure, clad in sumptuous scarlet and mounted upon a mule – a sponge soaked in vinegar and encased in the peel of an orange held to his nose to keep off the smell of the surrounding throng – could often be seen riding from his splendid palace to Westminster Hall, attended by numerous liveried servants crying out, 'Make way for my Lord's Grace!' It was natural that the King should turn to Wolsey when, tired of Catherine of Aragon, who had given him a daughter but no living son – and obsessively worried by the biblical text: 'And if a man shall take his brother's wife, it is an unclean thing ... They shall be childless' – he set his mind upon a divorce. With this end in view, Wolsey approached the Pope; but the Pope was Clement VII who had recently been driven from Rome by Queen Catherine's uncle, the Emperor Charles V. An indecisive man, distracted by his recent misfortunes, Clement delayed giving the answer which Wolsey and the King required. Henry was by now in love with one of his Queen's ladies, the pert, excitable and sensual Anne Boleyn, great-granddaughter of Sir Geoffrey Boleyn, hatter, mercer and Lord Mayor of London who had bought Blickling Hall

Henry VIII's chief minister, Cardinal Thomas Wolsey

in Norfolk and had created of himself a country gentleman. The longer he was obliged to wait, the more determined the King became
to make Anne Boleyn his Queen and the mother of his longed-for
heir. By the end of 1532, soon after Wolsey's disgrace and death,
Anne was known to be bearing Henry's child; and in January the
next year they were married, secretly and in haste. Soon afterwards
Thomas Cranmer, a married man of reformist views, was confirmed
as Archbishop of Canterbury in succession to Queen Catherine's
friend, William Warham; and, in early May, an ecclesiastical court
convened by Cranmer decreed that the King's marriage to Catherine
of Aragon was null and void.

The Pope responded by excommunicating the King, while the
King initiated the long process of legislation establishing the
principle, which several of his predecessors had endeavoured to
maintain, that the authority of the King of England was independ-

Numerous religious houses were dissolved in the reign of Henry VIII

ent of Rome and putting a stop to the revenues that customarily flowed from England into the capacious coffers of the Curia.

To support him in his endeavours to reform the relationship between the King and the Papacy without disturbing Roman Catholic doctrine – or the right of the King to the title Defender of the Faith which had been granted to him by Leo X for a pamphlet he had written on the errors of Protestantism and which in the abbreviated Latin form of 'Fid Def' or 'FD' is still seen on coins of the realm – the King summoned Parliament which his father had called upon only six times in twenty-three years. Parliament obligingly passed the Act of Supremacy which declared the King to be Supreme Head of the Church of England.

The legislation of the Reformation, that religious upheaval which turned Roman Catholic England into a constitutionally Protestant country, was not unpopular with the people at large; nor was the Dissolution of the Monasteries which accompanied it. For years anti-clerical feeling had been growing in England and had been exemplified by the satisfaction caused by the fall of Cardinal Wolsey, that archetypal churchman, proud and pompous, who had amassed such immense riches from lay and ecclesiastical offices of profit.

For years, too, there had been a growing feeling in the country that most monasteries were fulfilling few if any of the functions for which they had been founded in the Middle Ages, that some of them – in the words of the official pronouncement decreeing inspection of the smaller foundations – were nests of 'manifest sin, vicious, carnal and abominable living'.

Objections were raised to the destruction of the monasteries in certain areas where they were still providing food and shelter for the destitute and travellers, as well as education for the sons of families in the surrounding parishes. In the troublesome north the uprisings known as the Pilgrimage of Grace caused the government disquiet for a time; but in the country generally the Dissolution caused little dismay, however disliked may have been the man employed to carry through the King's revolution, Wolsey's former secretary, Thomas Cromwell, son of a blacksmith who kept a public house at Putney, a man of extraordinary administrative ability and single-minded determination.

As the King's Vicar-General, Cromwell supervised the dismantling of the abbeys, the transfer of their properties and lands to the Crown, and their sale, through the Court of Augmentations, to the English gentry, rich speculators and, most commonly of all, to existing local landowners. Some of England's great abbeys still lie in romantic ruin, among them the Yorkshire abbeys of Kirstall, Jervaulx, Rievaulx and Fountains whose grounds have now been joined to those of Studley Royal. Many others were converted into private houses like Lacock Abbey in Wiltshire and Mottisfont in Hampshire. Several new houses were built in the grounds of dissolved monasteries, like Longleat, Sir John Thynne's mansion on the land of the priory of St Radegund. The money from very few was used for the endowment of charitable and educational establishments, as the reforming clergy had hoped, though Trinity College, Cambridge was founded by the King in 1546, not long after Christ Church, originally Cardinal's College, had been founded by Wolsey at Oxford following the demolition of the Augustinian St Frideswide's Priory.

By the time most of the abbeys had been transferred to their new owners in 1541, Henry VIII was fifty years old. The handsome,

lithe young man had become grossly fat; his fair features had coarsened; he inspired more fear than admiration. Anne Boleyn, increasingly petulant and hysterical, had been beheaded, condemned to death on charges of adultery with several men, including her brother; the King's third wife, Jane Seymour, had died in childbirth, having given him his longed-for son, Edward; the arrival in England of his fourth wife, the excessively plain Anne of Cleves, pressed upon him by Cromwell in pursuit of a German alliance, had led to Cromwell's following to the block the more agreeable figure of Sir Thomas More, executed for refusing to deny the principle of papal supremacy. The King's fifth wife, Catherine Howard, accused of being as unfaithful to him as Anne Boleyn was alleged to have been, was beheaded too. At last he found some comfort in the pain of his declining years in the company of his sixth wife, Catherine Parr, a good-natured, virtuous widow, who was kind to his children and sat with his ulcerated leg on her knee, discussing with him those recondite religious problems which had never failed to interest him.

For most of his reign, Henry VIII punished religious dissidents, whether Roman Catholic or Protestant, with impartiality. His son, Edward VI, however, the cold and 'lonely, clever boy' who succeeded him at the age of nine, was a convinced Protestant, surrounded by Protestant advisers, notably his uncle, Edward Seymour, Duke of Somerset, who had obtained for himself the 'name and title of Protector of all the Realms and Domains of the King's Majesty, and Governor of His Most Royal Person'. The King was still Defender of the Faith but that faith was now to be ever more avowedly Protestant, as defined by the 42 Articles which formed the basis of the 39 Articles, the cornerstone of the religious settlement of 1563 and still in force. Hugh Latimer, who had resigned the bishopric of Worcester in Henry's reign – after preaching forceful sermons urging on the Reformation which had brought him a prisoner to the Tower – returned to the pulpit to express views more advanced than ever. Thomas Cranmer, Archbishop of Canterbury, who had by now

given up his belief in transubstantiation, issued *The Booke of the Common Prayer and Administration of the Sacraments*, the use of which the Act of Uniformity of 1549 required in churches instead of the old Latin services. There being no abbeys left to plunder, the King's advisers turned upon chantries – shrines devoted to prayers for the dead – and seized their endowments. The Duke of Somerset himself lavished a large share of his accumulated riches upon the building of his huge palace, Somerset House in the Strand. To make way for this the Church of the Nativity of Our Lady and the Innocents was demolished and, to provide the stone for it, much of the Priory Church of St John Clerkenwell was blown up, little of the building being spared, apart from the south gate, St John's Gate. Attempts were made to take stone also from St Margaret's Westminster but the parishioners here drove the Duke's men off.

Elsewhere in the country, there were protests not only against the imposition of religious changes but also against the continuing

Catherine Parr and Henry VIII

**The Booke of the Common Prayer and
Administration of the Sacraments**

revolution in agriculture: in Devon and Cornwall people rebelled
against having to use a prayer book rather than the Latin forms with
which they had been so long familiar; and in East Anglia in 1547
there was a rebellion, led by Robert Kett, a well-to-do landowner,
against the growing practices of enclosing land for pasture and of
taking over the arable and common land on which poor country
people had for long relied for their subsistence. Kett's Rebellion
was soon suppressed and Kett and his brother hanged; but the
hesitant way in which Somerset had dealt with the growing crisis
enabled his rival, the Earl of Warwick, later Duke of Northumberland, to take over the government in the name of the King whose
health was failing fast.

Well aware that his fall from power was likely to be as sudden
as Somerset's if the King were to be succeeded by his half-sister
and rightful heir, Mary – the devoutly Roman Catholic daughter
of Catherine of Aragon – Northumberland endeavoured to secure

a Protestant succession with the ready complicity of the dying King. He hastily arranged for the marriage of his son to Lady Jane Grey, the King's cousin and a granddaughter of a younger sister of Henry VIII.

On the afternoon of 6 July 1553, King Edward died at the age of fifteen, poisoned by the medicines that his physicians had prescribed, with swollen legs and arms and darkened skin, his fingers and toes touched by gangrene, his hair and nails falling out. Although she fainted when told that he had nominated her his successor, and then tearfully declared that she had no right to the Crown since the Lady Mary was 'the rightful heir', Lady Jane Grey eventually gave way to the entreaties of her relations and to what she was persuaded to believe was the will of God.

The English people were, however, not so ready to submit. Nor was Mary. From her castle at Framlingham, she sent an order to the Council demanding the recognition of her rights; and in this she was supported even by the Protestant citizens of London, exasperated as they were by the corruption and mismanagement of the Duke of Northumberland who had pillaged the Church as ruthlessly as Somerset, lavishing fortunes upon Dudley Castle in Staffordshire and his London house in Ely Place. Mary marched into London unopposed. Northumberland was arrested and executed; and so was Lady Jane Grey after her father's implication in a rebellion against Mary led by the reckless conspirator, Sir Thomas Wyatt.

Mary was a virtuous and conscientious woman who would have been quite well suited to the quiet, orderly, innocent life of a nun. Unworldly and impressionable, she was unshakeably loyal to those few people she loved and to the religion which was the mainstay of her life. Her reign was to be remembered for the screams of the Protestants on the crackling fires of Smithfield, the deaths of Hugh Latimer, former Bishop of Worcester, and Nicholas Ridley, Bishop of London, burned alive at Oxford, of Cranmer also burned at Oxford, and of those three hundred others whose martyrdom was to be commemorated by John Foxe in a book which – with its strong implication that the English people had been chosen by God to fight against anti-Christ in the person of the Pope – was later to be considered so important a work that it was

ordained that copies should be available in all cathedrals, as well as in the houses of gentry and the upper clergy, for the edification of both servants and visitors.

Yet Mary who presided over this bloodshed was not cruel by nature. Obstinate and narrow-minded, she knew her way to God and could not conceive that there might be some other way. Men and women had to suffer for their refusal to accept it, not to be punished but to be saved. In vain did her husband advise her to be less rigorous, for political rather than religious considerations.

This husband was Philip II, King of Spain, a solemn, courteous young man whom she adored, the representative of all that she held most dear, her mother's country and her mother's faith. She longed to have a child by him so as to unite their two countries in blessed trinity with Rome. But all her hopes were in vain. Pregnancy after pregnancy proved illusory; her husband, eleven years younger than herself, returned to Spain, persuaded that his wife lacked 'all sensibility of the flesh'. She died in 1558 of cancer of the ovaries, miserable and unlamented, often in great pain, so fearful of assassination that she had taken to wearing armour, dragged by Spain into a war with France which resulted in the loss of Calais, England's last toehold on the Continent.

These were miserable times for England. The country was in economic decline, already plagued by those bands of unemployed, unruly vagabonds which were to present such an intractable problem throughout the coming years. Prices were rising; wages for most workers remained low, fieldworkers earning about twopence a day, the price they would have been asked to pay for a single rabbit. Men such as these looked with a kind of desperate hope to their new Queen, Anne Boleyn's daughter, Elizabeth, a pale, composed, simply-dressed Protestant girl who was said to have knelt down on the grass beneath an oak tree when told of her half-sister's death and her own accession and to have quoted in Latin the words from the 118th psalm, 'This is the Lord's doing. It is marvellous in our eyes.'

The court of Elizabeth I

Queen Elizabeth, twenty-five years old, was already a formidable personality. In a report to his master, the Spanish Ambassador in London described her as being 'incomparably more feared' by her advisers than her sister had been. She was also 'undoubtedly a very clever young woman' but 'extremely vain'. This was certainly true. She could read Latin and Greek with equal facility; she spoke French, Spanish and Italian as well as Latin and even a little Welsh. Roger Ascham, her tutor, had never known a pupil with a quicker apprehension or a more retentive memory. She could talk intelligently on any intellectual topic, and would spend three hours a day reading history. Yet, astute and alert as she was, she was susceptible to the most outlandish flattery. Even in old age when the smooth, reddish gold of her hair had given way to a wig and the remaining teeth in her wrinkled jaw were black and decayed, she expected the handsome men she liked to have about her court to tell her how beautiful she was, that they would die of passion for her, that they could not look upon her face for long for fear of being dazzled by its loveliness. Towards the end of her life the French Ambassador was disconcerted by her pulling open the front of her dress so that he could see her breasts and her belly 'even to the navel'.

She was exasperating as well as flirtatious, difficult and demanding, reluctant to make up her mind and constantly changing it, as eager to take all the credit for her government's successes as she was quick to shuffle the blame onto her ministers when things went wrong. Dictatorial and high-handed, selfish and ungrateful, she would irritably slap her ladies and even her ministers and councillors when they annoyed her. They all acknowledged her authority but often pursued policies in direct opposition to her wishes, keeping important documents from her sight and encouraging ambassadors to give her misleading reports. Fortunately they were for the most part themselves men of exceptional talent. Among them were Sir William Cecil, later Lord Burghley, industrious, trustworthy, a master of statecraft; Sir Francis Walsingham, the wily, brilliant organizer of a network of agents unparalleled in Europe; Sir Christopher Hatton, Lord Chancellor and skilled manipulator of the House of Commons. Her court was indeed a busy

hive of genius where intellectual gifts and gallantry were valued more than high birth, where even those who were its most decorative and dashing denizens, like the handsome and adored Earl of Leicester, and Sir Walter Ralegh, soldier, navigator, poet, historian and chemist, were men of exceptional ability. Musicians, artists and men of letters were encouraged at court as well as such adventurers as Hawkins, Frobisher and Sir Francis Drake who brought home great wealth from their voyages, delighting the Queen, a most exact not to say parsimonious accountant, by the enrichment of her coffers.

After the miseries of the previous reign it seemed, indeed, a golden age, the age of Christopher Marlowe and Shakespeare, of

William Shakespeare

Philip Sidney and Edmund Spenser, of Nicholas Hilliard, Thomas Tallis, William Byrd and Orlando Gibbons, and of Hakluyt's *Voyages and Discoveries of the English Nation* which described the adventurous explorations of the country's navigators, one of whose voyages – James Lancaster's to the East Indies – led to the establishment of the East India Company and the beginnings of the empire in India. Other voyages and discoveries were eventually to result in an even larger empire across the Atlantic in America. Yet the Queen was the patron rather than the begetter of the age. Her achievements have been exaggerated; her posthumous reputation is a triumph of propaganda over reason. The religious settlement, a compromise of views – while welcome to those who shared the Queen's own impatience with petty doctrinal squabbles – was as unacceptable to the extreme Protestants known as Puritans, as it

The Spanish Armada

was to ardent Catholics. Several times the Queen's life was in danger from conspirators, most notable amongst whom was the beguiling Mary Queen of Scots, daughter of James V of Scotland and, through a descent untainted by illegitimacy, great-grand-daughter of Henry VII. Once the King of France's wife, Mary Stuart was as troublesome to Elizabeth when living in Scotland as she was to be after she had been driven from that country by her Protestant lords who were outraged by her marriage to the Earl of Bothwell, murderer of her second husband, Lord Darnley. Queen Elizabeth did not shrink from having other conspirators tortured and then hanged, drawn and quartered as traitors. But Mary, as a queen and her cousin, she was reluctant to bring to trial; and it was not until her proven complicity in the plot of the Catholic would-be assassin, Anthony Babington, that Elizabeth consented to sign the Queen of

Scots's death warrant, afterwards characteristically blaming others for its precipitate execution at Fotheringhay Castle in 1587.

The following year the Queen's throne seemed under even greater threat from the Spanish Armada, an immense fleet of ships and tens of thousands of soldiers sent with the blessing of the Pope to overthrow the heretical Queen of England, to bring her country back into the Catholic fold and to prevent British troops interfering in the Netherlands where Protestant rebels were in revolt against their Spanish masters. But the Spanish galleys proved no match for the more manoeuvrable smaller British ships and, having suffered heavy losses, they were dispersed by storms. Driven further and further north, the survivors of the catastrophe were forced to sail round Scotland and down the coast of Ireland where many of those who clambered ashore in the hope of salvation were robbed, murdered or held to ransom.

The danger over, the Queen – who had made a speech celebrated for its stirring patriotism to the troops assembled at Tilbury – returned to her familiar cheese-paring, denying money to her crews and adequate support to her naval commanders. Yet all over the realm, immense sums were being spent on houses built by men who had been allowed to make vast fortunes through the remunerative offices, monopolies and licences granted them by the Queen or who had made fortunes by their own often shady speculations in trade and finance. William Cecil, Lord Burghley, granted the immensely profitable office of Master of the Court of Wards, owned Burghley House in Lincolnshire as well as Theobalds, a house nearer London which he was obliged to enlarge considerably 'by occasion of Her Majesty's often coming'. Christopher Hatton, the Queen's Lord Chancellor, all but ruined himself building Holdenby House in Northamptonshire which stood ready for ten years, full of servants vainly waiting for the Queen to come to stay. The Earl of Leicester, the Master of the Horse, spent as large a fortune upon Kenilworth Castle, Warwickshire. Several of those who had made fortunes in her time, either through profitable offices or by such commercial enterprise as the export of woollen cloth, turned to Robert Smythson, mason and architect, to advise them in their designs, as did Sir Francis Willoughby of Wollaton Hall,

**Little Moreton Hall, Cheshire, a characteristic
half-timbered manor house of the Tudor period**

Nottingham, Sir Henry Griffith of Burton Agnes, Humberside, and the Countess of Shrewsbury in that dramatic combination of the Gothic and the classical, Hardwick Hall, Derbyshire. Some of these houses were enormous, like Montacute near Yeovil, others, such as Sulgrave Manor, Oxfordshire, built in 1558 and occupied by members of the Washington family, were relatively small. Most were built of brick and stone; a few, like Little Moreton Hall, that astonishing black and white creation in Cheshire to which William Moreton added the jettied gatehouse in the 1550s, were of wood; many were in the shape of an 'E' – supposedly in flattery of Elizabeth – as was Charlecote Park where William Shakespeare is said to have been caught on a poaching expedition, tried in the great hall and flogged on order of the house's owner, Sir Thomas Lucy, subsequently to be ridiculed as Justice Shallow.

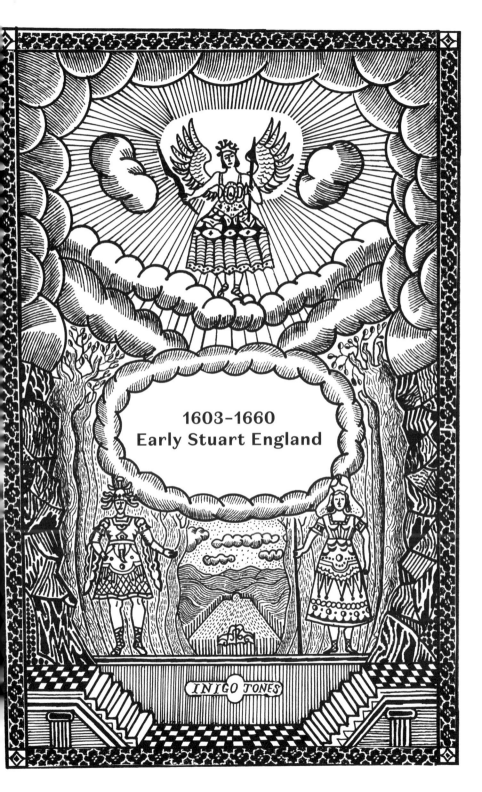

1603-1660
Early Stuart England

INIGO JONES

n her great bedchamber at Richmond Palace in the early morning of 24 March 1603 Queen Elizabeth turned her white and wrinkled face to the wall and died. Three hours later, as soon as it was light, a messenger galloped away to Edinburgh to inform her kinsman King James VI of Scotland, son of Mary Stuart, Queen of Scots, that he was King now, too, of England.

A few years later, after the arrival in London of this the first of the Stuart monarchs, Ben Jonson's *Masque of Augures* was performed in the recently completed Banqueting House in Whitehall. Nothing could have more fittingly symbolized the opening of a new age. The Banqueting House, designed by Inigo Jones and with a ceiling painted by Peter Paul Rubens, was the first purely Renaissance building to appear in London. While it was being built William Harvey, physician to St Bartholomew's Hospital, was working on the treatise which was to explain the circulation of the blood; William Gilbert's *De Magnete* had established the magnetic nature of the earth and founded the study of electrical science; John Donne, Dean of St Paul's, was writing the verse which proclaimed him the most notable poet of the metaphysical school; the Authorized Version of

the Bible, recently completed, was already becoming recognized as a masterpiece of English prose; Francis Bacon was revising the great works which propounded his radical system of philosophy; the group of English Puritans known as the Pilgrim Fathers had just sailed in the *Mayflower* to North America and had established a flourishing colony in New England at New Plymouth, Massachusetts.

The king who now ruled in the country which they had left was not a man to command respect. Described by the duc de Sully as 'the wisest fool in Christendom', he was certainly most learned and as pedantic as he was undignified. Conceited and slovenly, he spoke in the ' full dialect of his country' and in a very loud voice, expressing his opinions with an 'exasperating dogmatism'. Terrified of witches and naked steel, he hated the sea and pigs and wrote a diatribe against smoking, a habit now far more widespread than it had been in the recent past when a servant, seeing smoke emanating from Sir

Sir Walter Ralegh smoking a pipe, a common
habit in the early 17th century

Walter Ralegh's mouth, had thrown a pot of ale over him, supposing him to be on fire.

Instead of occupying himself with the evils of smoking and witchcraft, and with the handsome young men about his court, it was felt that the King should expend more thought upon the needs of the navy – much neglected since the end of the long war with Spain; upon the problems of Ulster – where Presbyterians were being settled on lands from which the Catholic Irish were being expelled; and upon the growing discontent in England of Puritans and Catholics alike. In 1605 there had been a plot, engineered by Catholics, to blow King James and his ministers up in the Houses of Parliament where Guy Fawkes had planted barrels of gunpowder in the cellars, a ritual search of which is still made by the Yeomen of the Guard before the State Opening of Parliament.

It was, however, not so much the Catholics as the radical Protestants whom the King saw as the 'chiefest enemies' of his authority and most of whose requests for reforms in the Anglican Church he firmly turned down at the Hampton Court Conference of 1604, rejecting their demands for changes in the government of the Church by bishops and in the prayer book, though agreeing to a new translation of the Bible which eventually appeared as the King James or Authorised Version in 1611.

His authority as King, James I insisted, was exercised by the ancient doctrine of divine right. He held that all his subjects should obey him as God's lieutenant on earth. Even women were required to kneel when presented to him; and Parliaments were regarded as mere instruments of the royal will, summoned to give their assent to royal decisions and to grant the money the government needed for the administration of the realm. Naturally most Members of Parliament were resentful of the low esteem in which the King evidently held them and the menial role in government to which he seemed determined to relegate them. More and more insistently, they were claiming the right to be consulted on important affairs of state, not to direct policy but at least to have a say in its formulation.

At odds with his first Parliament over money matters, the King dissolved it and contrived to manage without another for ten years,

Guy Fawkes planted barrels of gunpowder in the
cellars of the Houses of Parliament, 1605

raising money by selling peerages and baronetcies. He was driven to summon Parliament again in 1621 by shortage of money, but the unresolved disputes over the Members' right to be consulted as to the purposes to which the finances the King demanded were to be put, soon resulted in further quarrels; and once more the King sent them home, complaining of their insolence, resolute in his determination that Parliament should not presume to take more power into its hands than he deemed appropriate, that its functions should mainly be limited, as they had been in the Middle Ages, to voting the monarch the finances necessary for the conduct of the affairs of the realm. King James died soon after this last quarrel with his Parliament, leaving his son, Charles I, to cope with a problem which was to be resolved only by his own violent death.

Charles I had many admirable qualities but he inspired more respect than affection. His grave reserve, fastidious constraint and lack of humour were barriers to intimacy that all but a very few found it impossible to cross. His slight stammer, which in another man might have been appealing, was in him merely a defect which made it the more difficult for him to put strangers at their ease, seeming to emphasize the atmosphere of melancholy that surrounded him, a melancholy so well conveyed in Van Dyck's *Charles I in Three Positions* that when Bernini saw the portrait he described the countenance depicted as a countenance 'doomed'. 'Never,' the sculptor said, 'never have I beheld features more unfortunate.'

Charles was a studious rather than an intelligent man. He understood books better than people, and seemed incapable of making that kind of contact with his subjects which had ensured such popularity for the young Elizabeth I. With Parliament his dealings were from the start disastrous. Believing no less firmly than his father in the divine right of kings, he treated Parliament with a shy and distant reserve which seemed like contempt. Its Members, increasingly Puritan in sympathy, regarded both him and his foreign Catholic wife, his intimate friend, the Duke of Buckingham, as well as his High Church allegiance and his foreign entanglements, with the utmost suspicion. When asked to vote him the usual import duties for life, they declined to do so, granting them for one year only. The King responded by dissolving Parliament, collecting the

Van Dyck painted a triple portrait of Charles I

customs duties which had been denied him, raising a forced loan and threatening those who refused to pay with imprisonment. Compelled once more by shortage of money to call another Parliament in 1628, he found himself faced by a formidable opposition led by Sir John Eliot whom he had arrested and thrown into the Tower, but not before he had been forced to accept a Petition of Right which forbade the levying of taxes without parliamentary consent,

and not before his dear friend, the Duke of Buckingham, had been murdered.

After Parliament's dissolution, Charles managed by various financial expediences to survive for eleven years without calling another until 1640 when, having tried to impose his High Church practices north of the Tweed, a rebellious Scottish army marched into England. Another Parliament was now essential; and so the Members of what was to become known as the Long Parliament assembled at Westminster.

Immediately they ordered the arrests of the Earl of Strafford, the King's most ruthlessly efficient minister, and of William Laud, his Archbishop of Canterbury, 'a little low red-faced man of mean parentage', in the words of one of his many enemies, unimaginative and outspoken, sometimes irritable and often rude, a passionate upholder of High Church doctrines. After the King had been obliged to consent to the execution of Strafford – who was later followed to the scaffold by Laud – the drift into violent conflict between Crown and Parliament was much accelerated. A whole series of measures were introduced by the Long Parliament limiting the authority of the Crown while increasing its own. These measures were passed without undue difficulty; but plans for religious changes revealed wide differences of opinion among Members. So did a Militia Bill which proposed the transfer of military command from the Crown to Parliament, and a Grand Remonstrance – brought forward by John Pym and other leaders of the House of Commons – which urged radical reforms in the Church, including the curbing of the power of bishops, and the replacement of the King's counsellors by ministers approved by Parliament. This was too much for the King to tolerate. Having hesitated too long, he now went too far. Leading a party of swordsmen, he marched to the Commons to arrest Pym and four other Members. When he arrived there, he discovered that 'all the birds [were] flown'. They had escaped to the City where the authorities refused to deliver them up. War was now inevitable; and on 22 August 1642 in a field near Nottingham King Charles unfurled his standard beneath a glowering sky.

At that time there were scarcely more than a thousand men at his command; and many of those who had declared their allegia-

nce shared the reluctance of Sir Edmund Verney – shortly to be killed fighting for the King in Warwickshire – who declared, 'I do not like the quarrel and heartily wish the King would yield.' Many who might have supported the King, if only out of the simple loyalty displayed by Verney, hung back: it was harvest time for one thing; and, for another, the King was still making overtures to Parliament as though he hoped, even now, to reach a compromise. Men were reluctant to jeopardize their future by openly declaring their support of a cause which might at any moment be abandoned or betrayed by a man so widely distrusted because of his underhand dealings and prevaricating manner. But then Parliament declared that all men who did not support it were 'delinquents' and that their property was forfeit. This meant that those who would have been happy to stay neutral were virtually obliged to fight in their own defence; and men whose fortunes might have been lost had Parliament won, now undertook to raise troops to fight for the King in whose victory their own salvation might be secured.

If self-interest provided the spur for this early surge of support for the Royalist cause, other reasons, no less vital, played their part in swelling the numbers of men who eventually decided to throw in their lot with the King. It was not only that the King's majesty was considered by many to be sacrosanct. There was also the strong feeling that King Charles was the defender of the true Church, as he himself contended, anxious as he was to steer a steady and true course between the rocks of popery on the one hand and Puritanism on the other. He had read with admiration Richard Montague's *Appelo Caesarem* which identified popery with tyranny, and Puritanism with anarchy, and which concluded 'popery is originall of Superstition; puritanisme, the high-way unto prophaneness; both alike [are] enemies unto piety.' This stated the King's own views precisely. He had abhorred the priests of his Roman Catholic wife; he regarded with even more distaste the opinions of the Puritan landowners and merchants in the House of Commons and the Puritan preachers whose disrupting and often rabidly Protestant sermons could be heard all over London. It was his belief, no less than it had been his father's, that an attack on the bishops was an attack on the King. Moreover, while the Civil War was never prim-

arily a class struggle – the gentry were fairly equally divided – there was an undeniable fear among many of the King's supporters that the lower classes would use this opportunity to turn upon their masters, that the predominantly Puritan merchants and shopkeepers of the towns were intent upon upsetting the structure of power to their own advantage, that the King's opponents represented rebellion and chaos as opposed to law and order. These feelings were strongest in the north, except for the industrialized parts of Yorkshire and Lancashire, in the West Midlands and Wales, and in the West Country. Parliament, on the other hand, derived its strongest support from south-east England and London. But there were no clear lines of division. Hundreds of families were split in their loyalties; many changed from side to side with the fortunes of war; while thousands of country people found themselves drawn into the conflict on the side that their landlords and masters ele-

The King's men, or Cavaliers

cted to support. Thousands more were not too sure what all the fuss was about or did not really care what government they lived under so long as they could plough their fields and go to market. Only three men in every hundred took an active part in the conflict; and some did not even know there was a conflict at all. Long after the first battles had been fought, a Yorkshire farm labourer, when advised to keep out of the line of fire between the King's men and Parliament's, learned for the first time that 'them two had fallen out'.

Largely because of their preponderance in cavalry, it seemed at first that the King's men, or Cavaliers, as they consequently became known, would triumph; and had the commander of their horse, the King's young nephew, Prince Rupert of the Rhine, been less impetuous, they might well have won an important victory in the first indecisive battle at Edgehill. Thereafter the fortunes of the Royalists began to decline and the tide turned in favour of the

Parliamentarians or Roundheads as they were known because of their close cropped hair which was in marked contrast to the flowing locks of the Cavaliers. The stout and stolid Earl of Essex whom the Parliamentarians had placed in command of their army, was eclipsed by men of far more outstanding talent, by John Hampden, the influential Member of Parliament for Buckinghamshire, who was mortally wounded at Chalgrove Field, by the cavalry leader, Lord Fairfax, by Henry Ireton, the young Nottinghamshire lawyer who was one of the King's most implacable enemies, and, above all, by Ireton's father-in-law, Oliver Cromwell, a clumsy farmer from Huntingdon with heavy-lidded eyes, a face marred by warts and a large nose, Member of Parliament for Cambridge, and recognized by both sides in the conflict as a man of unswerving fixity of purpose and powerful, self-confident patriotism. 'His linen was plain and not very clean,' wrote a Member of Parliament who heard him speaking in the House of Commons for the first time; 'and I remember a speck or two of blood upon his little band which was not much larger than his collar. His hat was without a hat band. His stature was of a good size, his sword stuck close to his side; his countenance swollen and reddish; his voice sharp and untunable, and his eloquence full of fervour.'

'Pray, Mr Hampden,' another Member had once been asked by a colleague intrigued by Cromwell's roughskinned face with its conspicuous mole beneath his lower lip and his generally dishevelled appearance, 'Pray, who is that sloven?' 'That sloven,' Hampden had replied, 'that sloven whom you see before you hath no ornament in his speech; but that sloven, I say, if we should ever come to a breach with the King, in such a case, I say, that sloven will be the greatest man in England.'

So it proved to be. By his defeat at Marston Moor, the King lost the north; at Naseby he lost most of his army; and after the battle of Preston, it became ever more clear that he would lose his head. This he did on a scaffold outside the windows of the Banqueting House on a bitterly cold January day in 1649; and Oliver Cromwell, who had signed the death warrant of the royal 'Tyrant, Traitor, Murderer and Public Enemy', became, indeed, the greatest man in England.

The execution of Charles I outside the Banqueting
House, Whitehall, on 30 January 1649

Dealing ruthlessly with his other enemies, he imprisoned or shot mutineers in his army; crushed without mercy a rebellion in Ireland; routed the Scots who had proclaimed Charles I's son their King; won a final victory over his enemies in September 1651 at Worcester; constructed a fleet with which Admiral Blake defeated the Dutch; suppressed the Levellers who, led by John Lilburne, proposed a radical political programme not at all to his taste; and furiously dissolved the so-called Rump, the ineffective remnant of the Long Parliament that had survived a purge by one of his officers, Colonel Thomas Pride, a London brewer's drayman, who had arrested or excluded over a hundred dissident Members.

Cromwell replaced the Rump with an assembly largely chosen by himself; but this lasted a few months only, and in December 1653, by an Instrument of Government, he became Lord Protector of the Commonwealth of England. Ruling increasingly by decree, he instituted direct military rule by dividing the country into eleven districts commanded by major-generals.

Severe as Cromwell's rule was, it was a generally benevolent despotism which allowed a large measure of intellectual freedom and religious toleration, permitting the Jews to return to England. But it was also a joyless one which witnessed the wanton destruction of numerous treasures in churches and cathedrals throughout the country on the grounds that they were 'graven images', condemned to destruction, like the heads of the lovely medieval statues and the painted windows in the Lady Chapel at Ely Cathedral.

When the Lord Protector died, and was succeeded by his son, Richard, the regime began immediately to collapse. One of his generals, George Monck, later Duke of Albemarle, occupied London, and arranged for new parliamentary elections. The Parliament thus elected in 1660 resolved the crisis by asking the late King's son to return from his long exile in France as King Charles II.

The experiment with republicanism was over. Parliament proclaimed that 'according to the ancient and fundamental laws of this kingdom, the government is, and ought to be, by king, lords and commoners'. Yet, although a king was once more to sit upon the throne, the struggle for power had ended only superficially in the monarchy's favour. There was to be no return to the absolute rule

Oliver Cromwell, the Parliamentary general
who became Lord Protector in 1653

of the king. Just as the father had been defeated, so too might the son be. Parliament had established not only its right to financial control but also its right to be consulted on foreign policy and religion as well as trade and domestic affairs. In the future the problem for the monarch was not how to defeat Parliament but how to influence the rival political parties that alternately controlled a majority of its seats, until the monarch was seen to be above the strife altogether.

The Rise and Fall of Empire

From the Restoration of the Monarchy (1660) to the England of today

1660–1834
Empire and Industry

he shouting and joy expressed by all' at King Charles II's restoration to the throne was, so Samuel Pepys recorded in his diary, 'past imagination'. There were fireworks and bonfires and dancing in the streets; church bells rang and cannon roared as the King rode into the capital accompanied by an immense retinue of gentlemen in doublets of cloth of silver and velvet coats, of footmen in purple liveries, and soldiers in buff uniforms trimmed with silver lace. Not only royalists but all except the most diehard republicans welcomed the return of the monarchy, and they were not to be disappointed. The new King showed himself anxious to placate his former enemies as well as to reward his friends. They were given offices at court and in government impartially; and the protection of an Act of Indemnity and Oblivion was extended to everyone except those who had signed Charles I's death warrant and a very few others.

The curtains of reopened theatres rose upon comedies by William Wycherley, Congreve and Dryden. The King himself founded two theatre companies in Covent Garden where Inigo Jones's piazza and his church of St Paul's had been built some thirty years before; and he became, either personally or through his friends, one of London's

**The coronation procession of Charles II, who
was restored to the throne in 1660**

greatest benefactors. He laid the foundation stone of the Royal
Hospital, Chelsea, which was designed by Christopher Wren whose
first work, the Sheldonian Theatre, had recently been completed at
Oxford. He had the Queen's Chapel, opposite St James's Palace,
refurnished for his Portuguese wife, Catherine of Braganza. He extended the royal aviary, the site of the present Birdcage Walk, and
he improved Constitution Hill which is believed to have got its
name from his habit of taking walks there. He began a new palace
at Greenwich which, designed by Inigo Jones's pupil, John Webb,
is now the Royal Naval College; and at Windsor he employed the
architect, Hugh May, to rebuild the State Apartments where the
delicately painted ceilings by the Neapolitan Antonio Verrio and the
richly carved cornices and frames by Grinling Gibbons were much
admired by the King, whose taste for the exuberant and sensuous
style known as Baroque had been formed in Paris and Versailles.
He granted land in the area known as Soho after the ancient hunting cry, to his friend Henry Jermyn, Earl of St Albans, who was also
given several acres in St James's where a highly fashionable area
was developed including The Mall, Pall Mall, and several other streets around St James's Square, all named after members of the
King's family or servants.

West of this development, Hyde Park and Green Park were made into royal parks; while André Le Notre, whose work the King had admired in France, was commissioned to layout afresh St James's Park where Charles's tall, graceful figure could often be seen strolling about with his dogs and mistresses. Le Notre was also employed in laying out Greenwich Park where Wren was asked to design the Royal Observatory for the Astronomer Royal, Sir John Flamsteed.

It was the King's interest in scientific matters which induced the diarist and virtuoso, John Evelyn, to suggest that the groups of scientists and philosophers who met regularly at Gresham College to discuss the 'Advancement of Natural Science' should be formally instituted as the Royal Society. Among the Society's members, apart from Wren, Evelyn and Flamsteed, were John Aubrey, the antiquary; Robert Boyle, the physicist and chemist; Sir William Petty, the founder of population statistics; John Locke, the philosopher; and Isaac Newton, the greatest scientist of his age. Nothing, indeed, could have better illustrated the transformation of English society – the emphasis upon science and secular political philosophy at the expense of theological disquisition and religious enthusiasm – than the King's granting official recognition to the Society by its royal charter and his approval of its purposes by his attendance at the Society's meetings. Such patronage did not go uncensured; and when the Great Plague of 1664–5, the fearful climax of a series of epidemics, claimed thousands of victims in London, and when, soon afterwards, much of the City of London was destroyed by a raging fire, there were those who claimed that these dreadful visitations were God's angry punishments of a people steeped in sin and preoccupied with 'blasphemous questionings'.

The Great Fire presented the authorities with an opportunity for building the kind of Italianate city with wide streets and spacious piazzas proposed by John Evelyn. The opportunity was lost; but there did emerge among the ruins of the old city several beautiful churches, livery halls and other buildings by Christopher Wren and his assistant, Nicholas Hawksmoor, as well as Wren's masterpiece, St Paul's Cathedral.

The Great Fire of London

Worship in most of these churches was now conducted in accordance with the Anglican rites which Archbishop Laud had favoured and was accompanied by the music to be heard in the Chapel Royal at St James's Palace where the young Henry Purcell – soon to be hailed as the finest composer his country had ever produced – was then a chorister.

The King himself was not a devout man. He could be seen in his chapel asleep during the sermons or gazing fondly at some wanton mistress, or, on one occasion at least, kneeling to receive Holy Communion with three bishops on one side of him and three illegitimate sons by three different women on the other. Yet, while making fun of Nonconformists, and having scant sympathy with John Milton – champion of the Puritan revolution whose later works, written at this time, are imbued with despair – or with John Bunyan – author of *The Pilgrim's Progress*, begun in prison where he languished for refusing to accept the new regulations against Dissenters – the King strongly advocated leniency to-

wards Catholics and, pending parliamentary approval, promised to use his royal prerogative to relieve them of the restrictions under which they laboured. In 1672, when Parliament withheld its consent, he arbitrarily suspended the penal laws altogether. Parliament intervened, passing the Test Act which, besides requiring office holders to receive the Anglican communion, obliged them to repudiate the Catholic doctrine of transubstantiation.

Religious differences came to a head when Charles II died and, leaving no legitimate heir, was succeeded by his brother, James II, an avowed Catholic. An enthusiastic and tirelessly energetic adulterer, James had few other vices, apart from an impenetrable obstinacy, but his virtues were not attractive ones. Sincere but self-righteous, a firm friend but a 'heavy enemy', industrious but unimaginative and humourless, his principal objects in life were the conversion of England to Roman Catholicism and the establishment of a monarchy on the model of Louis XIV's. And after the defeat of rebel forces led by one of Charles II's illegitimate sons, the Duke of Monmouth, and the savage punishment of the survivors by the Lord Chief Justice, George Jeffreys, the King set his mind to the realization of his objectives. He admitted Catholics into his large army and into the universities; and in 1687 he issued his Declaration of Indulgence suspending the penal laws against them. Seven bishops who defied an order to read this declaration in all Anglican churches the following year were prosecuted and acquitted to tumultuous rejoicing; and after the birth of a prince threatened a Catholic dynasty, an invitation was sent by seven leading statesmen to William of Orange, James's Dutch nephew, a grave, shrewd Protestant and the husband of Mary, James's daughter by his first wife.

William landed at Torbay on 15 November 1688 and marched upon London as James's few supporters deserted him and he himself fled to France. The Glorious Revolution was thus achieved without bloodshed; and William and Mary jointly accepted the Bill of Rights which, excluding any Roman Catholic from the succession, confirmed the principle of parliamentary supremacy and guaranteed free speech within both the House of Lords and the House of Commons. On their acceptance of this Bill, William and Mary were crowned jointly in Westminster Abbey; and, in the defeat

of what was taken to be Roman Catholic despotism, the age of constitutional monarchy, of a monarchy with powers limited by Parliament, began. The revolution which brought about this shift in power has been, and continues to be, variously interpreted. For the nineteenth-century historian, Lord Macaulay, it was the most important event in modern history, ensuring that England was spared the revolutions that were to break out in other European countries. Later historians have tended to question its credentials as a revolution at all, either because ordinary people were only incidentally involved in it or because it was bloodless, though it led to bloodshed in Scotland where William III's troops fought the Jacobites, as supporters of James II and his heirs were known, and in Ireland where William defeated them at the battle of the Boyne in July 1690. Yet certain it is that after 1688 Parliament had to be summoned every year and not just when the monarch needed its help. The Crown still had formidable rights, not least in the choice of government ministers; but the struggle for power had taken a decisive turn in Parliament's favour.

For years the English had been at loggerheads with the Dutch from whom they had seized New Amsterdam in 1664, renaming it New York. Rivals in trade as well as in colonial expansion, the Dutch had also been exemplars to English merchants, providing them with models for the English banking system and the financial operations conducted at the Royal Exchange which had recently been rebuilt to the designs of Edward Jarman after the destruction of the earlier building in the Great Fire.

Now the Dutch were to be the allies of the English in the War of the Spanish Succession, a European war vigorously promoted by King William III in his determination to foil Louis XIV's attempt to place his grandson upon the Spanish throne. The War lasted for thirteen years, and by the time it was over both William and Mary were dead; Mary's sister Anne had become Queen; and the Duke of Marlborough had been rewarded for his splendid victories

The window tax drove many to brick up windows

on the Continent by the grant of the royal manor of Woodstock where John Vanbrugh, architect of Castle Howard and Seaton Delaval, built Blenheim Palace. To help pay for the cost of the war the window tax had been introduced, a tax resulting in the bricked-up windows still to be seen in the walls of many eighteenth- and early nineteenth-century houses. By the Treaties of Utrecht which ended the war in 1714, the year of Queen Anne's death, France ceded

to England much of her territory in North America, while the English also obtained various islands in the West Indies and a monopoly of the South American slave trade, as well as Gibraltar and Minorca as part of their share of the dismantled Spanish Empire. England, or Great Britain as she had become by the Act of Union with the Scots in 1707, had emerged from the war as a world power. She had also emerged as a trading nation with rapidly expanding resources and ever-growing export markets not only for textiles, for long the staple product of English workshops, but also for raw materials and for newer manufactures, from the output of foundries to weapons, tools and household goods. Industrial output was soaring. The merchant marine increased from 3,300 vessels in 1702 to 9,400 in 1776, and trade with the colonies created the largest free trade area in the world. Those working hard in England to supply this market were poorly paid, but prices were also low and remained so until the 1760s; the average worker in both town and country was better off, if only slightly better, in the middle of the century than he had been at the beginning.

At the same time the population of the country, still mainly employed in agriculture, was growing fast. In 1600 there had been about four million people in England and Wales. By the end of the century this number had risen to about 5,500,000, by 1780 to some 7,500,000 and by 1800 to nearly nine million. London's population of 375,000 in 1650 rose to some 575,000 by 1700 and to almost a million by 1800, when it was not only the biggest town in England but the biggest in the world.

Towards the end of September 1735, Sir Robert Walpole moved into the house which had been granted to him as First Lord of the Treasury, Number Ten, Downing Street. A tall, stout, good-natured, rather coarse Norfolk squire, who never entirely lost his provincial accent though he had been to Eton and King's College, Cambridge, Walpole had by then become an indispensable minister of the Crown, indeed the first Prime Minister, a title which was not, how-

ever, officially recognized until later. He was a Whig, that is to say a member of the ruling oligarchy of men whose authority was based on their ascendancy in local government and whose influence had helped to secure the succession of the German Protestant King George I, Elector of Hanover, upon the death of Queen Anne, his distant relative, none of whose many children had survived. The Whigs' rivals, the Tories – whose name like theirs was originally an obscure term of abuse and whose supporters often described themselves as the Church party since they were warmly regarded by the Anglican squires of the shires – had become associated with the Jacobites, supporters of the claim of King James II's progeny, and so were anathema to George I, who clearly preferred Hanover to England, never troubled to learn much English, and was content to leave the government in the capable if not over-scrupulous hands of Sir Robert Walpole, an astute businessman and political manipulator whose acumen restored public confidence in the government after the bursting of the 'South Sea Bubble', the disastrous failure of a joint-stock company formed to trade, mainly in slaves, with Spanish America.

The people as a whole, as well as the King, satisfied that the law was reconciled with liberty, were content to see the country governed in the name of the House of Hanover, by Whig ministers supported in office by Whigs in Parliament, a Jacobite rising in 1715 being easily suppressed. There was another Jacobite rebellion in 1745; but, although this caused alarm for a time, when an army led by King James II's grandson, the Young Pretender, 'Bonnie Prince Charlie', marched down into England from Scotland, the rebels soon lost heart because of their lack of support, turned back at Derby, and in a battle at Culloden, near Inverness – the last land battle to be fought in Britain – were slaughtered by the King's son, the Duke of Cumberland.

There was discontent in these years, of course, and widespread poverty: it was the age of Hogarth's *Gin Lane*; of the warnings of Henry Fielding, the novelist and Bow Street magistrate, that if spirit drinking continued at its present rate there would soon be few poor people left to drink it; of the underworld of Gay's *Beggar's Opera*; of lunatics chained and mocked in Bedlam; of prisoners

Sir Robert Walpole moved in to Number Ten, Downing Street in 1735

starved in Newgate; and of a savage penal code that condemned all kinds of malefactors to death by hanging.

But it was also the world of Handel and Canaletto, of Thomas Gainsborough and Joshua Reynolds, of Thomas Gray and Oliver Goldsmith, and of Richard ('Beau') Nash, master of ceremonies at Bath where the architect John Wood and his son were providing the city with such masterpieces of neo-classicism as the Circus and the Royal Crescent. It was, in fact, a world now inescapably associated with the term Georgian, a word not used in this sense until the beginning of the next century but signifying an elegant style of architecture and decoration strongly influenced by the

buildings of the ancient Romans and Greeks. The Grand Tour – that continental journey which was an essential part of a gentleman's education in an age when the universities were at a low ebb – was introducing the rich to the glories of Renaissance architecture and to the works of such Italian masters as Andrea Palladia and Vincenzo Scamozzi, whose influence on English taste was to be so profound. Sir Robert Walpole himself built his Norfolk country house, Houghton Hall, in the grand Palladian style; and this was to be followed by numerous other great country houses whose owners and architects had been inspired by Italian models encountered on the Grand Tour, among them Colen Campbell's Stourhead, Lord Burlington's Chiswick House, west of London, Holkham Hall built for Thomas Coke, later Earl of Leicester, and Hagley Hall designed by Sanderson Miller for the first Lord Lyttelton. Other houses were built by men of more humble birth who had made fortunes in India, like Claremont, designed for Robert Clive by Lancelot 'Capability' Brown – whose landscaping transformed the parks of so many country houses – and Sezincote, built in the Indian manner by Samuel Pepys Cockerell for a brother who had been in the service of the East India Company.

The British Empire in India and elsewhere was much increased by the victories of the Seven Years' War against France. By his triumph at Plassey in 1757 against the pro-French Siraj ad-Dawlah, ruler of Bengal, Robert Clive had established British ascendancy in Bengal; by his defeat of the French at Quebec two years later, James Wolfe had won Canada; and by the Treaty of Paris, which brought the war to a close in 1763, Brita in was seen as the world's leading colonial power with foot holds in Africa and islands in the West Indies as well as dominions in north America and Asia.

Robert Walpole, ill-suited to leading a government in time of war, had long since died; and the victories owed as much to the brilliant statesmanship of William Pitt, Earl of Chatham, the Prime Minister, as they did to the generals in the field. George I had also

Led by Bonnie Prince Charlie, the Jacobites were
defeated at a battle at Culloden, 16 April 1746

died and had been succeeded by his son, George II, who, towards the end of his life, was content to leave the government largely in the hands of his ministers. This was a policy not to the taste of his grandson, George III, an honest and kindly man with a most obstinate sense of duty, ill-advised by his mother and his 'dearest friend' and chief minister, the handsome and unexceptional Earl of Bute, to exercise to the full such royal powers as remained to him, particularly in the choice of ministers and in the exercise of patronage, the right to control the appointment to various offices, above all to offices presented to Members of Parliament, by which the Crown could manipulate voting in both Houses.

George III's attempts to rule through the 'King's friends' rather than through the Whig oligarchy and the Cabinet, the committee of the leading members of the government, which the Whigs controlled, soon led the well-meaning King into difficulties. One of his most scurrilous and effective opponents was the demagogue, John Wilkes, the 'most wicked and agreeable fellow' whom William Pitt had ever met. A profligate rake of great intelligence who charmed even Samuel Johnson, Wilkes was both a Member of Parliament and founder of the *North Briton*, a waspish periodical which the government attempted to suppress. Expelled from Parliament, he was three times re-elected by the defiant constituents of Middlesex; and by the time the American rebels had challenged the authority of King George III's government by their Declaration of Independence of 4 July 1776, Wilkes, together with Charles James Fox and Edmund Burke, had become one of the most outspoken opponents of government policies in the House of Commons.

Provoked by the government's persistent determination to tax their colonies and to oblige them to accept imported tea from the surplus stocks of the East India Company, the American rebels had first protested by tarring and feathering royal officials; then, disguised as Mohawks, by hurling chests of tea into Boston harbour. Eventually they demonstrated their determination to resist the royal troops by force of arms. Although a large proportion of Americans remained loyalist in sentiment, and although the King's troops won most of the battles fought in the War of Independence, the idea that the British army could subdue a continent at

such a distance from its own shores was, as the Adjutant-General put it, as 'wild an idea as ever controverted common sense'. After the surrender at Yorktown in October 1781 of General Lord Cornwallis to George Washington and his French allies, victory for the United States was assured.

The year before, London had been the terrifying scene of the worst riots in English history when an anti-Catholic demonstration, representing an age-old prejudice against papists as probably traitorous adherents of a foreign religion, was exploited by political activists, criminal gangs and workers with grudges against 'the wage-cutting blacklegs' of Roman Catholic Irishmen. At least 700 people lost their lives and the damage done to property was incalculable. 'Such a time of terror,' Samuel Johnson told Mrs Thrale, 'you have

In defiance of the Tea Act, American rebels hurled
chests of tea into Boston harbour

The Duke of Wellington

been fortunate in not seeing.' After the suppression of the riots – which George III threatened to put down in person at the head of his Guards since the magistrates appeared to be too frightened to do their duty – there were familiar calls for the establishment of a professional police force, and for various measures designed to repress a possible rebellion of an unruly working class. These calls were repeated a few years later when it was feared that repercussions from the Revolution in France would disturb the stability of England. It was at this time that Parliament passed the Combination Acts forbidding the forming of two or more people into a union for the purpose of obtaining a wage increase or better working conditions. But it was from the Revolution's heir, Napoleon Bonaparte, who threatened the country from without, rather than from such English working-class revolutionaries as the Luddites, who smashed the machines which were putting men out of work, that the real danger to the country came; and, while a series of towers – known as Martello Towers, after the tower at Cap Martella

where British troops had fought in Corsica – were built along the southern and western coasts, urgent efforts were made to bring the navy up to a strength capable of resisting the French invasion forces. After Lord Nelson's brilliant victories over the French fleet, culminating in his triumph at Trafalgar in 1805, there was no reason to fear a French invasion. Nor, after his final defeat at Waterloo in Belgium in 1815 at the hands of the Duke of Wellington and Marshal Blucher, was there any reason to fear Napoleon himself who died in captivity on the island of St Helena in 1821.

To tease the Duke of Wellington, it used to amuse George III's eldest son to extol his own prowess in leading heroic cavalry charges at Waterloo. 'In my life,' the Duke complained, 'I never heard so much nonsense and folly and so many lies in the same space of time.' This imaginative liar had been appointed Regent in 1811 when his father, suffering from the rare disease known as porphyria, displayed symptoms of insanity; and so the Regent gave its name to that exuberant style known as Regency, a neo-classical style based on Greek rather than Roman and on Egyptian and Chinese models. It was a style that might, indeed, have been specifically designed for the flamboyant and extravagant Regent himself who became King George IV on his father's death in 1820.

Exasperating as Wellington so often found the unpredictable 'blackguard', George IV, the Duke was forced to conclude that he was not only 'devilish entertaining' but 'a most magnificent patron of arts.' There was, indeed, scarcely a notable writer or artist of his time that George IV did not encourage and support. Even Byron, who joined in the general vilification of his selfishness, extravagance and lazy dissipation, had to admit that the King, that 'leviathan of the *haut ton*', had an impeccable taste in literature. He never lost an opportunity to praise the work of Sir Walter Scott and kept a set of Jane Austen's novels in 'every one of his residences'. As a lavish patron of English artists, he bought paintings by John Constable, sat for Nathaniel Dance, Cosway and Reynolds, commissioned works from Gainsborough, Stubbs, Hoppner, Romney and scores of other painters and sculptors, including Thomas Lawrence whose fine portraits of Napoleon's enemies now hang in the Waterloo Chamber at Windsor Castle – and Canova whose splendid and

colossal marble statue of Napoleon himself, presented by the King to Wellington, can now be seen at the Wellington Museum, Apsley House. Others of George IV's acquisitions now hang in the National Gallery, whose foundation in Trafalgar Square owes much to the King's enthusiastic support and whose imposing portico came from the Prince's sumptuous residence, Carlton House, in Pall Mall.

The rest of this grand house was demolished in the King's lifetime, Carlton House Terrace being built upon its site and in its gardens. At the same time the King's favourite architect, John Nash, was commissioned to build an even finer palace to take its place. This new palace, Buckingham Palace, was not finished until long after the King was dead. But George IV did live to see the realization of most of Nash's marvellous designs for Regent's Park and Regent Street in which he took the closest interest. He also saw to completion Nash's gorgeous Brighton Pavilion which took the place of an earlier Graeco-Roman-style seaside house and was decorated and furnished for him in an Oriental style of exotic grandeur. Its cost, as the Princess de Lieven said, was 'really incredible'; yet, even so, was meagre when compared with the sum lavished upon the reconstruction of Windsor Castle where, year after year from 1823 to 1830, with cavalier disregard of the sums allocated by Parliament, armies of workmen under the direction of Jeffry Wyatville laboured to give the Castle its present appearance of solid yet romantic grandeur that has made it one of the most distinctive monuments in the world.

George IV concerned himself not only with the arts. In the sciences too, his patronage was eagerly sought and gratefully welcomed. He was President of the Royal Institution and bestowed knighthoods on both William Herschel, the astronomer, and Humphry Davy, the chemist and inventor of the safety lamp, one of those many English scientists who were helping to make Britain the workshop of the world and playing their essential part in that social and economic transformation known as the Industrial Revolution.

In 1775, when the Industrial Revolution was gathering momentum, Adam Smith, the political economist, was elected a member of The Club. On its foundation, at the instigation of Joshua Reynolds, some ten years before, The Club had been a predominantly literary

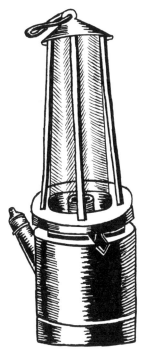

Humphry Davy's safety lamp

institution with Samuel Johnson and Oliver Goldsmith among its more distinguished frequenters. But as the years passed, its membership began subtly to change, scientists being admitted as well as the literary men, critics, and dramatists who had attended its meetings in the past. England was changing, too. In the country, men and women were beginning to leave the handlooms in their cottages to sit at wooden machines in workshops; towns were slowly growing; windmills and watermills were disappearing and tall chimneys were pouring forth a thick black smoke over the surrounding fields. Within twenty years of Dr Johnson's death, William Blake was writing of the 'dark, satanic mills' whose high brick walls were the prisons of the poor. By the time of Blake's death in 1827, James Hargreaves had invented the spinning frame which he named after his wife, Jenny; Richard Arkwright had set

up his own spinning machines in his large factory in Derbyshire; Henry Cort had revolutionized the manufacture of iron; Edmund Cartwright had invented the power-loom; James Watt's steam engines were grinding malt in Whitbread's Brewery; Richard Trevithick's steam-carriage had run between Leather Lane and Paddington, and George Stephenson was experimenting with the locomotives which were to culminate in the *Rocket*, capable of racing along at thirty miles an hour.

Pioneered by the Duke of Bridgewater, whose waterway between his coalmines at Worsley and Manchester was opened in 1761, canals were being dug by armies of men known as navigators or navvies all over the country where they still form a network of in land waterways from the Grand Union Canal and the Grand Junction Canal to the Ellesmere and Manchester Ship Canals at whose junction at Ellesmere Port is the Boat Museum where some of the ships that used to carry goods on them are preserved. Before the century was over there was not a large town in England which was not on a canal or within fifteen miles of one, some towns owing their very existence to the new waterways. Stourport in Worcestershire, for example – a town of some 4,500 inhabitants with ironworks, carpet-weaving factories and tanneries – had been developed because of the importance of its site at the junction of the Stour, the Severn and the Staffordshire and Worcester Canal.

Road transport was also being transformed: John McAdam, a magistrate and road trustee born in Scotland in 1756, had introduced new methods of drainage and surfacing; turnpike trusts, of which there were over nine hundred by the 1830s, had improved thousands of miles of roads by the erection of gates and bars and the collection of tolls by keepers, many of whose little houses, such as the one at Folly Bridge in Oxford, are still in existence; and hundreds of bridges had been built. Among the most remarkable of these were the world's first iron bridge built in 1779 by the ironmaster, Abraham Darby, across the Severn in Shropshire at the place known as Ironbridge – where several museums vividly recreate the area's industrial past – and the Menai Suspension Bridge built by the Scottish engineer, Thomas Telford, in 1825. This was the forerunner of the Clifton Suspension Bridge planned in 1829-31 by

Isambard Kingdom Brunel, designer of the *Great Britain*, the first ocean-going steamer with screw propulsion, which now lies in dock at Bristol.

Many of those travelling across these new bridges had little notion of the miserable lives led in the slums and factories of the growing towns. There were, to be sure, factories where the conditions of work were considered exemplary. For instance in that gloomy area of the Midlands known as the Black Country – where the restored bottle kilns of the Gladstone Pottery Museum at Longton provide a vivid impression of the work once undertaken there – Josiah Wedgwood's employees lived under their master's firm paternalistic care in a model village, Etruria, which had been especially built for them. And in Birmingham, whose population had risen from about 12,000 at the beginning of the eighteenth century to 45,000 in 1800, an American visitor to one of the town's factories found 'no mark of ill-humour' among the hundreds of persons employed there. Yet there were other places, factories, mines and sweatshops, where the conditions were appalling, where children where employed as well as women and were pushed into tubs of cold water to keep them awake during their interminable hours of labour.

In the earlier years of the nineteenth century there were protests and uprisings, riots against the Corn Laws – which had been passed by Parliament in 1815 to protect British agriculture and maintain the level of rents by charging high duties on imported grain – and demonstrations against the savage punishments imposed upon machine-breakers whose activities, it was feared for a time, might provoke a national revolution. In 1819 in St Peter's Field, Manchester, a large crowd of people, many of them distressed handloom weavers attending a rally in support of parliamentary reform, were charged by mounted troops who killed eleven of them and wounded hundreds more in what became known as the Peterloo Massacre in ironic allusion to the battle of Waterloo. In 1820 a group of radicals meeting in a stable loft in Cato Street conspired to murder the entire Cabinet while they were having dinner and to carry off the heads of the Home and Foreign Secretaries in bags. Betrayed to the authorities, five of the ringleaders were hanged. They were spared

being drawn and quartered because of public sympathy; but even so the hangman was attacked in the street and almost castrated. Ten years later, in protests against low wages and farm machinery, there were serious riots all over England as gangs of men with blackened faces, sometimes in women's clothes and often carrying flags and blowing horns, cut down fences, destroyed machinery and burnt down ricks and barns. Men who declined to join in the rioting were thrown into village ponds; and parties of yeomanry called out to suppress it were attacked with pick-axes and hatchets. When the risings were at last brought under control, several rioters had been hanged, well over 600 sent to prison and 500 sentenced to transportation, nearly all to the Australian colonies. Soon afterwards, in 1834, in the Dorset village of Tolpuddle, six farm labourers who had administered oaths to their fellow workers were arrested and charged with having administered 'illegal' oaths for 'seditious' purposes. Although trade unions had been legalized ten years before, the men from Tolpuddle were arraigned under an eighteenth-century Mutiny Act and, like the rick-burning rioters, were sentenced to transportation.

The furious protests which these punishments aroused could not be ignored, however; and it was clear that a new age, later to be known as the Age of Reform, had begun.

The 'Peterloo Massacre' of 1819 in Manchester where
several demonstrators were killed by yeomanry

1830s–1900
The Age of Reform

t was only yesterday,' exclaims one of Thackeray's characters, 'but what a gulf between now and then. *Then* was the old world. Stage-coaches, more or less swift riding horses, packhorses, highwaymen ... But your railroad starts a new era ... We who lived before railways and survive out of the ancient world, are like Father Noah and his family out of the Ark.'

Certainly, since the opening in 1825 of the first public railway, the Stockton and Darlington, the whole tenor of English life as well as the English landscape had been transformed. By 1852 there were only a few market towns and coastal resorts without a railway station; twenty years later all these had been provided with one. By 1875 nearly five hundred million passengers were being transported each year, and all London's main termini, except Blackfriars (1886) and Marylebone (1899), had been completed. Some were horrified by the change the railways brought about. The Duke of Wellington, who survived until 1852, complained that 'people never acted so foolishly as we did in allowing for the Destruction of our excellent and commodious [post roads] in order to expend Millions Sterling on these Rail Roads ... the vulgarest, most indelicate, most

injurious to Health of any mode of conveyance' that he had seen in any part of the world. Yet there were advantages as well as regrets. The railways helped the new towns to grow, and as they grew, so did the capacity of their inhabitants to enjoy fresh food: the sponsors of the London to Birmingham line's London terminus at Euston noted with pride that it was built on the site of a warren of cowsheds and cow-cellars from which the nearby households had previously been supplied with tainted and watered milk instead of the fresh milk that could now be brought in from the country. Moreover, as it became possible for people to travel beyond the confines of the enclosed communities they had rarely been able to escape before, they discarded their previous suspicions of the outside world and learned both that their fellow countrymen were much like themselves and that social justice, as the reformers encouraged men and women to think, was a national concern.

Among these reformers was William Cobbett, who died in 1835. A farmer's son and former sergeant-major, whose *Rural Rides* is a vivid and revealing portrait of England in the early nineteenth century, Cobbett had become one of the most influential of the anti-establishment radicals. His contemporary, Jeremy Bentham, a leading proponent of parliamentary reform, had found wide support for his belief that legislation must aim to achieve 'the greatest happiness of the greatest number;' and Robert Owen, the Welsh social reformer whose sympathetic management of the New Lanark cotton-mills had induced other owners to introduce more enlightened methods into their own concerns, had strenuously supported the Factory Act of 1819 which gave a measure of protection to children employed in industry. Thereafter the pace of reform had begun hesitantly to quicken. As Home Secretary from 1822, Robert Peel had introduced a series of measures lessening the severity of the criminal law, which as late as 1819 had still recognized as many as 223 offences as punishable by death; and in 1829 he saw the Metropolitan Police Bill, which proposed the creation of the capital's first professional police force, pass both Houses without serious opposition, paving the way for a paid constabulary in all the counties of England. In 1829 Roman Catholics were at last granted full civil and political rights by the Roman

Sir Robert Peel's professional police force, the 'Peelers'

Catholic Emancipation Act. And, at the general election of 1830, the Whigs under Lord Grey were returned to power after more than half a century in opposition and turned their minds to the problem of parliamentary reform.

Although the Tories were traditionally opposed to the measure, it had long been generally conceded that parliamentary reform was overdue. Only about one person in every hundred had a vote; and, while several large towns such as Manchester – whose population with that of Salford had already risen to 84,000 by 1801 – had no representative in Parliament at all, there were several places far smaller which had two. There were also various so-called rotten or pocket boroughs, like Satton which was no more than a park and

Dunwich which had for centuries been submerged beneath the North Sea. These were mostly in the hands of landowners who nominated Members as they chose. George Selwyn, for example, the rich and witty Member for Gloucester who would travel any-where to watch a good hanging, owned the pocket borough of Luggershall in Wiltshire. He agreed to sell it to General Simon Fraser when it seemed that Fraser, who was standing for Inverness-shire, might be defeated by his opponent, Lord George Gordon. Fraser consulted his father, Lord Lovat, who in turn spoke to the Duke of Gordon, Lord George's elder brother. Between them they decided it would be cheaper to buy Selwyn's seat than to bribe all the electors of Inverness-shire. So Luggershall was bought and presented to Lord George Gordon who accordingly agreed to withdraw from Inverness-shire so as to leave the field clear for Simon Fraser. Nobody regarded the transaction as anything out of the ordinary.

It was in order to prevent such deals by the abolition of rotten boroughs, to grant seats to new towns which lacked them and to give the vote to certain additional holders of property that Lord Grey's government brought forward their modest Reform Bill in 1831. The member of the government mainly responsible for draft-ing the Bill was Lord John Russell, son of the Sixth Duke of Bedford, a clever and persuasive little man whose heart was set on reform both political and educational. Despite a persuasive speech by Russell in the Commons, the Bill was defeated. Grey therefore resigned and appealed to the country; the Whigs were returned again with a large majority; and the Bill, somewhat amended, was again presented to the Commons who now passed it. The government could not, however, get it through the Lords; and it was not until Lord Grey went to see the King, George IV's brother William IV, that the problem was resolved. Grey proposed that the King should create a sufficient number of new peers to ensure the passage of the Bill. The King, naturally reluctant to do so – since such a measure would threaten the whole fabric of the Upper House – was saved from the necessity by the Tories' submission. Their leader, the Duke of Wellington, advised acceptance of the Bill which eventually became law in May 1832.

The next year a whole series of reforms were enacted. Many of them were proposed by the Seventh Earl of Shaftesbury, the indefatigable philanthropist in whose memory was erected the statue by Alfred Gilbert known as Eros at Piccadilly Circus and after whom Shaftesbury Avenue was named. Shaftesbury concerned himself with a wide variety of causes, from the plight of lunatics to the laws relating to the employment of women and children in factories and mines, from the treatment of chimney sweepers' climbing-boys to the education of the poor and the eradication of slums. It was, indeed, largely due to Shaftesbury's efforts that some of the worst abuses in society were brought to the attention of a generally complacent middle class.

While Shaftesbury was concerning himself with the plight of the English poor, other reformers were struggling to abolish slavery and to complete the work of William Wilberforce, the rich merchant's son and close friend of Pitt, who had done so much to kill the slave trade itself in 1807. Their efforts met with success in 1833 when – in the year that Shaftesbury's Factory Act made it illegal to employ children below the age of thirteen for more than forty-eight hours a week – slavery was abolished throughout the British Empire.

Much as was achieved by Lord Grey's government and those of his successors, Melbourne and Peel, radicals had cause to complain that progress was not proceeding fast enough and that some innovations were positively deleterious. The Mines and Collieries Act of 1842, it was admitted, went some way towards dealing with the exploitation of women and children in coal mines by pro-hibiting the employment of women underground as well as boys under ten. But the Poor Law Amendment Act of 1834 did little to ameliorate the miseries of the destitute. Before the passing of this Act, poor relief had been administered by the system known as the Speenhamland System from the place in Berkshire where the justices had originally devised it. By this method exceptionally low

Charles Dickens

wages had been supplemented from parish rates, a system which, far from relieving poverty, encouraged employers to keep wages low. The Poor Law which abolished it, however, instead of offering relief to paupers, by giving them sufficient money to survive in their own homes, forced them into workhouses, and was far from an agreeable alternative, since conditions in workhouses were deliberately rendered so unpleasant that most poor people did all they could to avoid entering them. Charles Dickens's description of workhouse fare as constituting 'three meals of thin gruel a day, with an onion twice a week, and half a roll on Sundays' – while not intended to be taken as exact – was not far from the truth; and the bowl of soup and small piece of bread which the poor boys are given in the large stone hall in *Oliver Twist* was not an unusual meal under a system by which children under nine years of age were dieted 'at discretion'.

There was widespread dissatisfaction with the new Poor Law and with the Reform Act which, while welcomed by the propertied middle classes, was a profound disappointment to radicals and the militant working class. There was dissatisfaction also with the failure of attempts to develop trade unionism; and this general discontent ensured that unrest continued throughout the 1830s and helped to increase support for the movement for political reform known as Chartism.

This movement took its name from a People's Charter drawn up in 1838 by a group of radicals who demanded of the government universal male suffrage and vote by secret ballot, equal electoral districts, annual parliaments, an end to property qualifications for Members of Parliament, and the introduction of salaries for them. Support for these six demands was loudly voiced at meetings held both by day and night all over the country. One such gathering at Halifax attracted a crowd of 200,000. 'It is almost impossible to imagine the excitement caused,' one Chartist wrote of these rallies. 'Working people met in their thousands and tens of thousands to swear devotion to the common cause ... The processions were frequently of immense length ... The meetings themselves were of a still more terrific character.' In 1839 there was a threat of a general strike; and later on that year when 7,000 men, mostly miners and iron workers, marched through the streets of Newport, Monmouthshire, demanding the release of a Chartist orator from the local gaol, soldiers opened fire on them and at least twenty-two were killed.

There were riots, too, in renewed protest against the Corn Laws whose effects were exacerbated by a series of poor harvests. In 1839 an Anti-Corn Law League was founded to denounce the Laws as benefiting landowners at the expense of workers; and speakers propounding the views of the League, and raising funds for its propaganda, travelled all over the country in the steps of Richard Cobden, a Sussex farmer's son who, in his own words, 'lived in public meetings', and John Bright, the son of a Quaker mill owner from Lancashire. In the opinion of a Tory landlord, expressing a general view, the League was 'the most cunning, unscrupulous, knavish, pestilent body of men that ever plagued this or any other

The unpopular Corn Laws worked in favour of rural landowners

country.' But it was a Tory Prime Minister, Robert Peel, who, after a poor harvest in England and the failure of the potato crop in Ireland, was persuaded in 1846 that the Corn Law must be repealed. The decision came too late. In Ireland, where potatoes were the staple diet, about a million people perished of starvation or disease and a further million emigrated, many of them to America where they nurtured a hatred of England shared by most of the Irish people who remained behind. The decision split the Tory party. Although he steered the repeal through Parliament, Peel was obliged to resign, and many of his followers joined the Whigs – now the developing Liberal Party soon to be dominated by the towering figure of William Ewart Gladstone while the remaining Tories, or Conservatives as they were now more generally known, regrouped themselves under Benjamin Disraeli, a Christianized Jew of mixed Italian and Spanish descent who had attacked the government's proposal to repeal the Corn Laws in a series of brilliant speeches. Disraeli poured such scorn upon Peel that his victim, a shy, awkward man with an aloof manner and an exces-

sive sensitivity to ridicule, was observed more than once to change colour dramatically as he listened, to laugh loudly and defensively in pretence of amusement, or to pull his hat down over his eyes and his nervously twitching face.

Upon Peel's resignation in 1846, the Liberal Lord John Russell became Prime Minister; and it was his government which had to deal with the continuing problems presented by the Chartists who were planning to organize a massive demonstration in London and to present a petition to Parliament containing even more signatures than the three million appended to an earlier petition of 1842. The demonstration was planned for 1848, the year of revolutions on the Continent where the King of France was forced to abdicate and the Austrian Empire and Germany were both in uproar. It was hoped by the Chartist leaders that revolution might break out in England, too. The Royal Family were advised to leave London for the safety of their house at Osborne on the Isle of Wight. Already the lamps outside Buckingham Palace had been smashed and shouts of '*Vive la république!*' had been heard. But Lord John Russell's government, of which the pugnacious Lord Palmerston was a senior member, stood firm. Immense numbers of police were brought into London; 150,000 special constables were enrolled; yeomanry regiments were called up. Feargus O'Connor, the Irish orator and journalist, a leading figure in the Chartist movement, urged the crowds to disperse. Another Chartist leader gloomily conceded that the government had proved too strong for the workers. Thereafter Chartism gradually declined. And Queen Victoria, in tears and shivering with fright before she left for Osborne, expressed her profound relief that the trouble was over, that the workmen, misled by professional agitators and the 'criminals and refuse of London', remained loyal after all.

Queen Victoria, who had succeeded her uncle, William IV, in 1837, was then twenty-nine years old, the mother of six children and the happy wife of Prince Albert of Saxe-Coburg and Gotha whom she manifestly adored. Although well instructed in her rights and duties by her first Prime Minister, Lord Melbourne, the Queen was not content to be a mere figurehead and interfered in the processes of government far more insistently than her ministers

Victoria and Albert with their children

thought seeming or the constitution allowed. An emotional and selfish woman, difficult, demanding and capricious, she was imperious, though innately shy, finding throughout her life official engagements unusually tiring as they not only bored her but made her nervous. Often she had to restrain herself from giggling. She had little cause, however, to be unsure of herself in the presence of ministers, for she had many varied talents of her own. Her intellect was limited, but she had an astonishingly good memory. She was hardworking, well informed and shrewd. Her judgements, however, were never tentative, never in doubt. Incapable of lying or dissembling herself, she was also incapable of understanding that there were degrees of reprehensibility. A thing was right or it was wrong; a person was good or bad; and, once her mind was made up, she had absolute confidence in her opinion. She played the part of Queen and Empress with an instinctive and formidable distinction.

The monarch had, and has, every constitutional right to make suggestions; yet Queen Victoria often overstepped the limits of constitutional propriety, writing to her royal relations on political matters without the knowledge of the Cabinet, corresponding with generals without reference to the War Minister, and with former prime ministers behind the backs of their successors, threatening to abdicate if the government pursued policies of which she disapproved, on occasions actively supporting and encouraging the opposition, and reacting angrily at any hint of criticism. Although Prince Albert is justly given credit for helping to guide the Queen towards the creation of a new English monarchical tradition which placed the throne above party, he, too, was prone to the kind of constitutional indiscretion encouraged by his adviser, Baron Stockmar, who was of the dangerous opinion that the monarch was the 'permanent Premier' and the prime minister merely 'the temporary head of the Cabinet'.

Although never much liked in the country at large, Prince Albert was generally respected by the Queen's ministers; and after his premature death, which laid her prostrate with grief, it was considered only appropriate that his memory should be honoured by the Albert Memorial in Kensington Gardens, the highly expensive monument in which the statue of the Prince is seen holding the

The Crystal Palace at the Great Exhibition of 1851

catalogue of the Great Exhibition of 1851 which he had done so much to organize and encourage.

The Great Exhibition of over 100,000 objects from all over the world was held in a specially constructed Crystal Palace designed by Joseph Paxton on the lines of a conservatory he had created for the Duke of Devonshire at Chatsworth in Derbyshire. The Crystal Palace was afterwards removed to Sydenham where it served as the first home of the Imperial War Museum whose new premises – part of the old Bethlem Royal Hospital in Lambeth – now contain a model of the original Palace burned down in 1936. The Exhibition held here in 1851 was a notable success, attracting over six million visitors and making a handsome profit which, with the help of funds voted by Parliament, paid for the transformation of a large part of

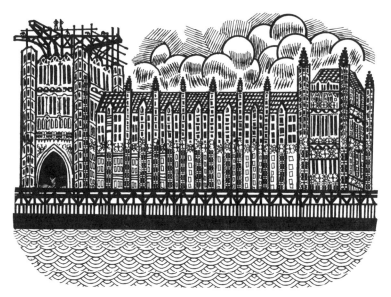

The Houses of Parliament were rebuilt in Gothic style in 1834

Kensington where Exhibition Road, Queen's Gate and Cromwell Road – all names chosen by Prince Albert himself – were built soon afterwards. Also built on land purchased by the Great Exhibition Commissioners in the 1850s were the Albert Hall, the Victoria and Albert Museum, the Natural History Museum, the Science Museum, and the Geological Museum.

At the same time the University Museum was built in Oxford. At the strong instigation of John Ruskin, whose *Stones of Venice* was published in 1851–3, this museum was built in the Gothic style, the style chosen also for the Houses of Parliament, rebuilt after their destruction by fire in 1834. Thereafter Gothic was selected for numerous churches, country houses and collegiate buildings throughout the country, from G. E. Street's Royal Courts of Justice in the Strand and William Butterfield's Keble College, Oxford, to Alfred Waterhouse's Manchester Town Hall and George Gilbert Scott's Midland Hotel, St Pancras Station.

When in 1831 work had begun on the huge Gothic Harlaxton Manor in Lincolnshire to the designs of Anthony Salvin and its

owner Gregory Gregory, there had been little enthusiasm for this style. The architect of the Gothic Houses of Parliament, Charles Barry, would have preferred to have submitted a Renaissance design; and when in the 1860s new government offices were required along Whitehall, Lord Palmerston received vociferous support when he insisted that they should be in Italianate rather than in the Gothic style, which Sir George Gilbert Scott at first proposed. But by the time Ruskin had resigned his Professorship of Fine Arts at Oxford in 1884 and retired to the seclusion of Brantwood he had succeeded in changing a whole generation's attitude to architecture. Despite the outrageous prejudice of some of his statements, he had ultimately convinced most of his countrymen that the Gothic style which he had so passionately championed – and which was so grandly exploited for the creation of Allerton Park, North Yorkshire – was a style far better suited than any other to reflect the glories of the British past. By his defence of J. M. W. Turner, whose work was at first derided by the critics, Ruskin had also taught the public to recognize the genius of the most original landscape painter of the nineteenth century; while by his advocacy of Holman Hunt, Millais, Rossetti and the other Pre-Raphaelites, he had encouraged a revolt against the conventional academic painting of the day.

A social reformer, as well as author and artist, Ruskin concerned himself also with national education, the organization of labour, the foundation of training schools, old-age pensions, and the building of decent homes for the working class. Moreover he supported the kind of industrial experiments advocated by William Morris whose revival of handicrafts and views of house decoration, as exemplified by the decorations and furniture in his own houses – the Red House in Bexleyheath, Kent, Kelmscott House, Hammersmith and Kelmscott in Oxfordshire – were revolutionizing English taste.

Many of Ruskin's reformist ideas were ridiculed in his time and dismissed out of hand by successive governments. Lord Palmerston, who was brought to power when the Conservative government of Lord Aberdeen revealed its incompetence during the Crimean War against Russia in 1854–6, was for most of his time in office preoccupied with foreign affairs, with the suppression of the

mutiny of the native soldiers of the Indian army in 1857, with the problems presented by the struggles for the unification of Italy and with the conflicts precipitated by the opium trade in China – a trade which a Parliamentary Committee had deemed it 'inadvisable to abandon since it engendered so important a revenue'. Britain's overseas possessions, of which the Queen was so proud and which covered so many thousands of square miles marked in pink on the maps of schoolroom walls, were still, after all, widely regarded as being held to serve the business interests of British merchants and manufacturers and to provide the mother country with raw materials, even though, since the loss of the American colonies, there had grown up a new conception of Empire as being not merely a means to riches through trade but a political organization of peoples involving responsibilities as well as rights.

From 1867, however, when Disraeli – who became Conservative Prime Minister for the first time the next year – was largely instrumental in pushing through the second Reform Act, which almost doubled the electorate, until 1894 when his rival, Gladstone, retired at the age of 84, the pace of reform, much of it inspired by the writings of J. S. Mill, equalled that of the Shaftesbury era. The Education Act of 1870 introduced universal elementary education; the Trade Union Act of 1871 gave unions legal status and a later Act the right to picket peacefully; the Ballot Act of 1872 made voting secret, putting an end to bribery and intimidation. Long overdue reforms were instituted in the Army by Edward Cardwell as Secretary for War from 1868 to 1874; in public health by Sir Edwin Chadwick; and in hospital administration by Florence Nightingale, who having trained in Prussia and France, had gone out to nurse the sick and wounded and badger the medical department in the dreadful hospitals of the Crimea. There were reforms also in land tenure and poor relief; in the constitution of the universities and in the treatment of prisoners.

From time to time the attention of public was diverted from this erratic march of progress by the outbreak of wars and the progress of events in the now huge British Empire. There was intermittent fighting along the frontiers of India whose imperial crown the Queen assumed in 1876; there was fighting in Afghanistan after

Florence Nightingale

the assassination of the British Resident in Kabul; there was trouble, too, in Egypt from whose bankrupt Khedive Disraeli bought a controlling interest in the Suez Canal on behalf of the government and presented the shares to the Queen, as though they were a personal gift, with the words, 'You have it, madam, the entire interest of the Khedive is now yours.' There was fighting in the Sudan where General Gordon perished attempting to evacuate Egyptian forces from Khartoum, and Kitchener at last established British authority by his victory at Omdurman. In Zululand a British force was destroyed at Isandhlwana; in South Africa peace came only after further humiliating defeats at the hands of the Dutch settlers, the Boers, had been revenged by General Roberts. And, as always, there was trouble in Ireland.

By the 1880s Gladstone had come to the conclusion that the demands for Irish Home Rule, that is to say, for an Irish parliament responsible for the island's domestic affairs, made by Charles Stewart Parnell and other Irish Members of Parliament, must be met. The Queen was horrified, writing to the Prince of Wales to express her dissatisfaction with her 'dreadfully Radical Government ... and

the way in which they truckled to the Home Rulers – as well as the utter disregard of all my opinions which after 45 years of experience ought to be considered.' She had never liked or trusted the Irish; and Gladstone's suggestion that she should spend as much time there as she did at her beloved Scottish home, Balmoral, was an absurd idea, just such a one as might have been expected from this 'wild incomprehensible ... half-mad firebrand'. If only Disraeli had lived all would have been different. But Disraeli had died in 1881 and now lay buried in the village churchyard near his country house at Hughenden.

Had he and his party wished it, Disraeli might have persuaded the Queen to regard Home Rule with less hostility. By his ingratiating tact and fulsome flattery, by the impression he gave of needing to consult her and have the advice of her astute mind, he contrived on occasions to change it. He recognized himself that he often 'laid it on rather thick' with his coaxing blandishments. But, as he said to Matthew Arnold, 'You have heard me called a flatterer, and it is true. Everyone likes flattery; and when you come to royalty, you should lay it on with a trowel.' But he never underestimated the Queen's astuteness; he grew genuinely fond of her – even though he declined to see her when he was dying on the grounds that she would only want him to take a message to Albert – and, in treating her with elaborate courtesy, he was behaving towards her as he did to all women he liked. Gladstone, a man of the utmost moral rectitude who hated dissembling, could not bring himself to treat the Queen in such a way. He addressed her, so she said, as though she were a public meeting and was quite incapable of following the advice of his wife who sensibly said to him, 'Do pet the Queen, and for once believe you can, you dear old thing.' But it was not in Gladstone's nature to do so. He was a man of remarkable political and administrative ability as well as a splendid and powerful orator. There was great nobility in his character; yet there was in his manner something of the pious humbug. In a telling comment the Liberal politician and journalist, Henry Labouchère, said of him that he did not object to Gladstone 'always having the ace of trumps up his sleeve, but only to his pretence that God had put it there'. It was to this aspect of Gladstone's character that the

Queen took exception; and when his Home Rule Bill was defeated by a combination of Conservatives and dissidents in his own party, the Queen accepted his resignation, and the Marquess of Salisbury as his Conservative successor, with unconcealed satisfaction. Upon Gladstone's death in 1898 she declined to express any grief. 'No, I did not like the man,' she declared with characteristic honesty. 'How can I say I am sorry when I am not?' It was left to her eldest son to pay the widow due respects: he kissed Mrs Gladstone's hand at the funeral and, to his mother's annoyance, played the part of pall-bearer. Three years later the Queen, too, was dead; and the age to which she had given a name died with her.

The term Victorian was already in use in 1875 when Victoria had over a quarter of a century to live. It has been taken to imply a regard for hard work and thrift, strict morality and family virtues; in one dictionary it is defined as 'exhibiting the characteristics popularly attributed to the Victorians, especially prudery, bigotry or hypocrisy'.

The Queen's eldest son, with whom she had so often found fault, and who now succeeded her as Edward VII, was unarguably a Victorian by birth but very far from being a Victorian by nature. He seemed, indeed, a highly appropriate figure to preside over the society that drifted – as apparently unconcerned as the *Titanic* steaming towards the icebergs of the north Atlantic – into war with the Germany of the nephew whom he so much disliked, Kaiser Wilhelm II.

1901–1990
The Twentieth
Century

he King who came to the throne in 1901 and who gave his name to the Edwardian era, is remembered for none of the staid Victorian virtues which might have been expected from a man born in 1841 but rather for his self-indulgence and extravagance, his enormous girth and gruff bonhomie, his fondness for good and expensive food, fast horses, pretty women, huge cigars, France and shooting on his Norfolk estate at Sandringham. His short reign, to quote R. J. White, 'lingers on the edge of subsequent darkness like a long summer afternoon, quietly punctuated by the popping of champagne corks, flavoured with cigar smoke, and accompanied by the distant strains of Elgar's *Pomp and Circumstance* march from the Guards' Band in the Park.'

For many English people, life in the years before the First World War was far from that associated with visions of *la belle époque.* Beneath the glittering surface of society there was widespread poverty, bitterness and unrest. Yet year by year, by slow degrees, reforms continued to come and the quality of life for the mass of the people gradually improved, with advances undreamed of a century before in medicine and housing, in technology and condit-

The early twentieth century saw both glittering nightlife
and poverty, bitterness and unrest

ions of work. Farming emerged from the agricultural depression
of the 1870s and 1880s; and in the towns successful strikes were
organized by the poorly paid and the exploited. Striking dockers,
for example, were promised the modest wage of sixpence an hour
which they had demanded; and when the match-girls at Bryant
and May's factory went on strike in 1888 against the dangerous,
ill-paid and squalid conditions of their work they won their case.
In that year a Local Government Act established county councils;
in subsequent years factory acts made further improvements in
conditions of work, housing acts eliminated some of the worst
slums, and education acts brought free schools and free school
meals within the reach of thousands of poor children. For the
better-off, scores of independent schools were founded to instil in
their pupils those 'religious and moral principles' and 'manly conduct' which Dr Arnold had required of his boys at Rugby, one of
those numerous so-called public schools, many of them founded
in the previous century, whose role in turning boys into gentlemen
was seen by their critics as one of the main foundations upon which
the indestructible English class system was based.

There were still those who agreed with the physician, Sir
Almroth Wright, that 'there are no good women, but only women
who have lived under the influence of good men'; but there were
far more who recognized that women had lived for far too long
with as few rights and as little freedom as the 'doll in the doll's house'
which Bella Rokesmith complains of being in *Our Mutual Friend* or
as Sally Brass's downtrodden maid in *The Old Curiosity Shop* who

is 'ignorant of the taste of beer, unacquainted with her own name (which is less remarkable) and [takes] a limited view of life through the keyhole of doors'. In the field of medicine, for example, after the admittance of Elizabeth Garrett Anderson to the Medical Register in 1865, and the establishment of the London School of Medicine for Women in 1876, the infiltration of women into what had previously been regarded as a male preserve was generally accepted. In 1882 a Women's Property Act at last enabled married women to own their own property; and while the militant feminist movement of the Suffragettes, the demonstrations and strikes of Mrs Pankhurst's Women's Social and Political Union, and such desperate protests as that of Emily Davison who threw herself beneath the King's horse at the Derby in 1913, were brought to an end by the War, votes were granted to women over thirty as soon as the fighting was over and to all women on the same terms as men ten years later.

In 1905 a general election brought the Liberals back to power under Sir Henry Campbell-Bannerman whose Cabinet included H. H. Asquith, the son of a Nonconformist wool-spinner from Lancashire, David Lloyd George, whose mother was the poor widow of a Welsh schoolmaster, and Winston Churchill, grandson of the Seventh Duke of Marlborough, all three of whom were to be prime ministers in their turn.

Campbell-Bannerman's government occupied themselves earnestly with reform, as did that of his successor, Asquith. More slums were cleared and towns replanned; labour exchanges were established and minimum wages fixed in certain industries; pensions were paid to the old; and, by the Trade Disputes Act of 1906, unions were granted protection from liability for losses caused by strikes. The Lords had looked askance at several of these Liberal measures without actually blocking them. But when Lloyd George, as Chancellor of the Exchequer – in an attempt to raise money for his government's reforms, as well as for rearmament against Germany – brought in his budget in 1909 proposing higher death duties as well as a land tax and a supertax on incomes over £3,000 a year, they rebelled. And it was not until after two general elections had been fought, and Edward VII's son, King George V, had been prevailed upon to agree to the creation if necessary of over 200 Liberal peers

The Suffragette movement campaigned
for women's suffrage

to outvote the Conservatives that the crisis was resolved. In 1911 the Parliament Act was passed, severely curtailing the powers of the Lords and establishing the Commons as the supreme legislative body. In that same year a National Insurance Act provided relief for the sick and the unemployed; and a salary of £400 was introduced for Members of Parliament who, soon afterwards, included men supported as candidates by trade unions. Already James Keir Hardie, a former miner and Secretary of the Scottish Miners' Federation,

had become leader of the Independent Labour Party, forerunner of a Labour Party dedicated to a socialist policy of 'common ownership of the means of production'; and Ramsay MacDonald, also Scottish, the illegitimate child of a maidservant and a ploughman, and one day to be the first Labour prime minister, had been elected to Parliament as Member for Leicester.

The problem of Ireland remained unresolved and apparently insoluble. After the failure of a second Home Rule Bill, relations between the Irish nationalists and the Protestants of Ulster, who were determined not to lose their identity in a Roman Catholic Ireland, went from bad to worse until the Government of Ireland Act proposed partition with separate parliaments for north-east and south. This solution provoked such resistance in the south that its twenty-six counties had eventually to be granted virtual independence from Britain, with the six counties of the north-east remaining part of the United Kingdom. This proved unacceptable to the Irish Republican Army and its supporters who demanded, and still demand, the withdrawal of British troops from Ulster and the establishment of a republic of the whole of Ireland.

Despite the quarrels, thousands of Irishmen joined the British Army when Britain declared war all Germany in August 1914 after the Kaiser's troops had invaded Belgium; and by November 1918, when the dreadful struggle was over, there were many Irish corpses among the million British dead. Lloyd George, who had replaced Asquith as Prime Minister at the height of the conflict, promised the survivors that he would undertake 'to make Britain a fit country for heroes to live in'. For a time it appeared that this promise might be fulfilled. But the post-war boom was over within two years and was followed by a long period of depression, strikes and hunger marches. By 1921 there were over two million unemployed. The next year Lloyd George was obliged to resign, never to return to office, and to witness the eclipse of the Liberals by the Labour Party as the main opposition to the Conservatives.

Britain declared war on Germany in August 1914,
leading to four years of trench warfare

He was succeeded by the Conservatives under Bonar Law, followed by Stanley Baldwin, a square-faced, pipe-smoking, seemingly
lethargic man, then by a Labour government under Ramsay Mac-
Donald, then in 1924 by Baldwin again.

In 1926 a General Strike was called in support of the miners
who, after its failure, were forced by hunger to return to work with
longer hours and lower wages even than before. Yet, outside the
mining districts, the strike seemed to have improved rather than
worsened relations between the poor workers and the well-to-do,
the 'two nations' into which Disraeli had described the country as
being divided in the previous century. The middle classes who had
volunteered to take the place of strikers to keep essential services
running had, for the first time, come to understand the nature of
manual work and to respect those who undertook it, while the
workers, brought into contact with people whose backgrounds
were so different from their own, were surprised to discover how
much in common they shared.

It was an opportunity for the 'lasting peace' for which the King
called. But, although Baldwin, too, was a moderate man, pressing
always for conciliation rather than confrontation, the opportunity
was lost. Legislation was imposed upon the unions that much reduced their powers; and largely as a result of their repressive
measures, the Conservatives lost their majority and had to give way
in 1929 to another Labour government which, after the American
slump, was faced with an economy close to collapse and three
million unemployed. After disagreements in the Cabinet over cuts
in unemployment benefit, this beleaguered Labour government
felt obliged to form a coalition government with the Conservatives and Liberals in 1931.

Unless they happened to come across some such 'hunger
march' as that of the unemployed shipyard workers who came down
to London in 1936 from Jarrow in Durham – where two-thirds of
the population was out of work – visitors to the south of England
found it hard to believe that the country was faced with any kind of
crisis, financial or otherwise. For this was the world of the cocktail
and the slow fox trot, of Noel Coward's *Hay Fever*, of Somerset
Maugham's *The Constant Wife*, of Sapper's *Bulldog Drummond* and

**Shipyard workers marched to London from Jarrow to
protest against unemployment in the North East**

Michael Arlen's *The Green Hat*, as well as that of the economist,
John Maynard Keynes, and of the socialist, Harold Laski, of Kingsley
Martin's *New Statesman*, of G. B. Shaw's *Intelligent Woman's Guide
to Socialism and Capitalism*, and of T. S. Eliot and W. H. Auden. It
was the day of the motor-car – there were already two million of them
on the roads by 1939 – and the age of the seaside holiday: Blackpool
alone had seven million visitors a year.

The architecture of the period reflected its mood. Scores of
hotels were being built like the Park Lane and the Mayfair both
completed in 1927, the Strand Palace of 1930 and the Dorchester

The 1930s were the days of the motor-car

of 1931. Hundreds of cinemas appeared at the same time, from grand picture palaces such as the Odeon in Kensington Church Street to the little cinemas of country towns, few of which now survive as cinemas, though many were converted into halls for playing bingo, a gambling game of eighteenth-century origin, which become extremely popular in the second half of the twentieth. Scores of theatres were going up too: the Saville Theatre in London, for example, in 1931; the huge New Theatre, now the Apollo, in Oxford in 1933. So were larger and larger shops. London's first Woolworth's was being built in Oxford Street in 1924, soon to be followed by numerous other stores of which D. H. Evans (1937) was a characteristic example.

To take shoppers and office workers home to their houses in the suburbs ever expanding around London – as they were round all other large towns – the lines of the underground railway were constantly being extended and new stations, such as those by Charles Holden on the Piccadilly Line to Hounslow, were being built in a style that evokes a vivid image of those days of the 1930s when Stuart Hibberd wore a dinner jacket to read the news at the recently built Broadcasting House, when George V's son, the future, unfortunate, King Edward VlIl, could have been seen dancing with Mrs Dudley Ward at the Embassy Club, when Ivor Novello's *Glamorous Night* was delighting audiences at the Theatre Royal, Drury Lane, and there were long queues outside cinemas showing Shirley Temple in *Curly Top*.

To most of these pleasure-seekers of the 1930s the economic problems of the country seemed far away. Indeed, by the middle of the decade politicians were informing them, in the words of Neville Chamberlain, Baldwin's Chancellor of the Exchequer and soon to become Prime Minister, 'that we have recovered in this country 80 per cent of our prosperity'. The story of *Bleak House* was over, he announced, and the people could now sit down to enjoy the first chapter of *Great Expectations*.

Soon afterwards the Italian Fascist dictator, Benito Mussolini, invaded Abyssinia and the German Chancellor, Adolf Hitler, reoccupied the Rhineland of which Germany had been deprived by the 1919 Treaty of Versailles, whose harsh terms had made a future European war almost inevitable. In 1938 German troops entered Austria; in 1939 they seized Czechoslovakia; then Hitler turned upon Poland; and Chamberlain, who had done all he could to avoid fighting by a policy of appeasement, was obliged to declare war on Germany, whose well-trained army crossed the Polish frontier on 1 September after Hitler had signed a non-aggression pact with Russia.

Chamberlain was not the man to lead his country in such a crisis; and Churchill, his First Lord of the Admiralty, took over as Prime Minister, directed the fortunes of his country with erratic brilliance for five years, and at the general election of 1945 was heavily defeated at the polls by voters anxious that Britain should

During the Second World War ration books were issued to every person

Winston Churchill

not return to the politics of the 1920s and 1930s when Churchill, as Home Secretary at the time of the General Strike, had misguidedly referred to the workers as 'the enemy'.

The leader of the Labour Party which now came to power – with an absolute majority in the House of Commons for the first time in its history – was Clement Atlee, a restrained, laconic man who might well have been mistaken for the manager of a small bank and whose great gifts were so well concealed by a veneer of imperturbable diffidence that Churchill is supposed, in a characteristic judgement nor intended to be taken seriously, to have described him as 'a sheep in sheep's clothing'.

His government – in which the reassuringly bulky figure of Ernest Bevin was Foreign Secretary, the ascetic Sir Stafford Cripps President of the Board of Trade, and the fiery Welsh orator, Aneurin Bevan, Minister of Health – set about their task with invigorating energy, introducing a series of Bills in fulfilment of promises to nationalize essential industries and the means of supply, to lay the foundations of what became known as the Welfare State and to bring back some measure of prosperity to a country where rationing was as severe as it had been during the war. The government also began to restore the havoc caused by air raids which had damaged or destroyed no fewer than 3,500,000 houses in London alone as well as laid waste such national treasures as Coventry Cathedral, which was rebuilt to the designs of Sir Basil Spence.

By 1951, the centenary of the Great Exhibition and the year in which the Conservatives under Winston Churchill were returned to power, so much had been done that the government decided to hold a Festival Exhibition on derelict land on the south bank of the Thames in Lambeth 'to demonstrate to the World the recovery of the United Kingdom from the effects of War in the moral, cultural, spiritual and material fields'. The press derided the pretension of this claim, but the Festival was visited by nearly ten million people; and the Royal Festival Hall – 'the first major public building in inner London designed in the contemporary style of architecture' – remains a fitting memorial to the enterprise. Subsequent public buildings on the South Bank, notably the Hayward Gallery and Denys Lasdun's National Theatre, have not been so well received.

For thirteen years after their re-election in 1951, the Conservatives were in power. They were years of growing prosperity; wages were far higher than they had been before the war though prices had risen very little; more and more people were buying cars and going on holidays. 'Let's be frank about it,' the Prime Minister declared in 1957, 'most of our people have never had it so good.' By the 1960s Britain was one of the world's leading industrial as well as nuclear powers.

This world was now divided between a communist east and a capitalist west, with various uncommitted nations hovering uneasily between the two and an international body with headquarters

The Festival of Britain was held on the South Bank, London, 1951

at New York, the United Nations, endeavouring to settle the differences between them. When in 1950 the communist North Korea invaded the South, which was supported by the United States, sixteen members of the United Nations, including Britain, sent troops to defend the South and helped to bring the war to an inconclusive end. In 1956 another war was brought to an end when – under pressure from the United States – British troops were obliged to withdraw from Egypt where, in alliance with France and in collusion with Israel, they had landed in an effort to bring about the fall of the Egyptian President, Gamal Abdel Nasser, who had recently nationalized the Suez Canal.

The Suez adventure, which brought about the fall of Anthony Eden, Churchill's successor as leader of the Conservative Party, was an anachronistic display of imperialism. Churchill had declared in 1942 that he had 'not become the King's First Minister

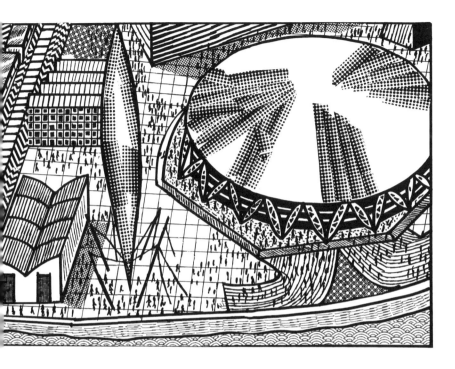

in order to preside over the liquidation of the British Empire.' Yet during the intervening years the Empire had dissolved all the same. India and Pakistan gained their independence in 1947, Burma in 1948; Newfoundland joined the Dominion of Canada in 1949; several former African colonies emerged into statehood. Soon few of Britain's old colonial possessions were left, and most of these were being claimed by other countries. Gibraltar, captured from them in 1704, was being claimed by the Spanish; Hong Kong, ceded by them in 1842, by the Chinese; the Falkland Islands, a crown colony since 1892, by the Argentinians whose army launched an attack upon them in 1982, an attack vigorously resisted by the Conservative Prime Minister, Margaret Thatcher, who – calling an election after the immensely expensive British victory – won another victory for the Conservatives, their most decisive for forty years.

Margaret Thatcher was the sixth Prime Minister the country had had since Eden had resigned in 1957 in favour of Harold Macmillan,

an almost theatrically patrician figure who, like his successor, the kind, modest and old-fashioned Sir Alec Douglas-Home, seemed peculiarly out of place in a country becoming known for its 'permissive society'. The governments of none of Mrs Thatcher's predecessors, neither those of the Labour leaders, Harold Wilson and James Callaghan, nor that of the Conservative Edward Heath, had succeeded in finding a satisfactory answer to the economic and industrial problems of the country or to the celebrated complaint of the American Secretary of State, Dean Acheson, that Britain had lost an Empire but not yet found a new role. It was an observation voiced also by the French President, General de Gaulle, who believed that Britain was too closely involved with the United States to make a satisfactory member of the European Economic Community established by the Treaty of Rome in 1957. Twice de Gaulle vetoed Britain's application for membership of the Community which she had declined to join upon its foundation; and it was not until January 1973, during the premiership of that zealous advocate of European co-operation, Edward Heath, that she was admitted to membership at last. Yet the British people remained equivocal about the Community.

By the beginning of the 1980s the English were falling behind in the world race. In 1964 they had produced more per head of population than any of the countries in the European Community except West Germany. In 1977 they produced less than any other except Italy. Had it not been for the discovery of oil in the North Sea the economic decline would have been even sharper. While those in work continued to prosper, unemployment was high and there were social as well as economic problems that seemed intractable, problems posed by increasing pollution, by crime and violence, by unassimilated immigrant communities, racial and class prejudice and the decay of inner cities, problems soon to be compounded by rising inflation.

Mrs Thatcher, single-minded and didactic, unswerving in her belief in self-reliance and what came to be known as privatization (of previously nationalized industries), was determined that Britain should lose as little as possible of her sovereignty, and that, to use her own words, the country should 'recover her self-confidence

Margaret Thatcher, Conservative Prime Minister from 1979 to 1990

and her self-respect'. In so doing Mrs Thatcher took on and defeated a string of opponents, both within her party, where she contemptuously referred to her critics as 'wets', and in the trade union movement, whose previously unbounded capacity for industrial action she subjected to stringent legal limitations. Her most formidable enemy on the left was the miners' leader, Arthur Scargill, who ultimately went down to defeat after a long and bitter strike that saw miners battling with mounted police in an attempt to halt the wholesale closure of collieries and the winding-down of the mining industry itself. Yet the truth was that the world was moving on from the labour-intensive heavy industries of the past in favour of a brave new world of computer-reliant service industries and independent small businesses, and Mrs Thatcher intended Britain to be at the forefront of the change. In a move little noticed at the time but full of symbolic portent for the future, in 1989 a Swiss-based British computer scientist named Tim Berners-Lee came up with the idea for something he called the World Wide Web which, he declared, was 'for everyone'.

1990–today
Into the New
Millennium

WINDRUSH

rs Thatcher's unshakable confidence in her own judgement deeply divided opinion, and never more so than in her determination to introduce a new form of local government taxation, angrily denounced as a medieval-style 'poll tax' in widespread demonstrations that soon tipped over into full-scale rioting. Alarmed that Thatcher's leadership was rapidly becoming a political liability, in December 1990 her own MPs removed her in a coup, replacing her with the comparatively little-known John Major, who went on to win an unexpected victory in the general election of April 1992. Major's period in office was dogged by deep divisions in the Conservative Party over Britain's relationship with the European Union, as the former European Community became after the 1992 Maastricht Treaty. Europe played an increasingly important role in British public life through the 1990s, despite the opt-outs Major had won at Maastricht from some of its more centralizing tendencies and the dramatic events of 16 September 1992, when international financial speculation forced Britain to withdraw from the European Exchange Rate Mechanism, a precursor to a unified European currency. Britain's ever-closer links to the Continent

were powerfully symbolized by the opening, in May 1992, of the Channel Tunnel, enabling direct rail links between London and Paris and ending Britain's physical isolation from Europe that had lasted since Neolithic times. British scepticism about the EU continued, however, even within the Labour Party, which was swept to power in 1997 under the leadership of the young and charismatic Tony Blair. Blair had hoped to take Britain into the Euro, the single European currency launched in 1999, but he was persuaded against it by his less sunnily-tempered chancellor and designated successor, Gordon Brown, who correctly gauged the lack of public support for the move. Opposition to the EU grew in stridency as the Euro itself began to fall apart in the 2010s under the strain of supporting the EU's poorer and less solvent members; ever-louder calls for a referendum on Britain's continued membership of the EU developed to the point where the Conservative Prime Minister, David Cameron, felt obliged to grant one in 2016. To his stupefaction, and that of Britain's erstwhile fellow EU members, the British people voted to leave the Union, in which they had never felt properly at home, and see how far the modern world would let them run their own affairs.

John Major

Other long-running sagas also moved to their climax as the millennium drew to its close. Peace finally came to Northern Ireland after two historic agreements, the 1993 Downing Street Declaration by John Major and the Irish *Taoiseach* Albert Reynolds, and Tony Blair's 1998 Good Friday Agreement with the major Northern Irish parties, which established a power-sharing executive with the previously unimaginable spectacle of Sinn Fein and their sworn enemies, Ian Paisley's Democratic Unionist Party, happily governing together. Even more remarkably, the IRA agreed to a complete ceasefire, though dissident republicans sought to undermine the peace process by launching a series of spectacular bomb attacks, including one in Omagh, in August 1998, which killed twenty-nine people, the single worst loss of life of the Troubles. Nevertheless, the success of the peace process was sealed in 2011 by a highly successful state visit by Queen Elizabeth II to the Republic of Ireland, unthinkable while the Troubles were still happening.

Tony Blair's landslide election victory in 1997, notable for the unusually high number of Labour women MPs it produced, ushered in a strikingly different style of politics. Building on the success of his predecessors in seeing off the power of the militant left-wing, Blair sought to remodel the Labour Party as 'New Labour' – smart-suited, media-friendly, prepared to work with big business, pragmatic and radical in its commitment to modernization. Blair had already persuaded his party to ditch Clause IV of its constitution, which had committed it to public ownership of the economy; his spruced-up party, shorn of its troubling connotations with the trade union strife of the 1970s, appealed to an electorate looking for a change after eighteen years of Conservative rule. With his informal 'sofa style' of conducting business, Blair made it clear that he represented a challenge to the traditional political establishment. Reform of the House of Lords was therefore an early priority: Blair ended the ancient right of hereditary peers to sit in Parliament, though he shied away from proposals to make peers elective, which would have given them a democratic mandate to rival that of the House of Commons.

Another ancient institution bowing to new trends was the Church of England, which in 1994 ordained its first women priests

and would in 2015 consecrate its first female bishop. The Catholic Church, which had no plans to follow suit, saw the move as a major obstacle to closer relations with the Church of England, opening its doors to that vocal minority of Anglican clergy who objected to the ordination of women and even allowing married former Anglicans to become married Catholic priests. Debate in the Church of England soon moved on to the even thornier question of the ordination of homosexual clergy, an issue that provoked deep divisions in the worldwide Anglican communion, where churches in Africa found it difficult to accept homosexuality itself, never mind among the clergy. Indeed the Church of England found itself lagging behind the state: civil partnerships between same-sex couples were introduced in 2005 and in 2013 Parliament went a step further by allowing gay couples of either sex to marry. Popular support for the move, despite the deep reluctance of the Churches to support it, was a sign of the extent to which the British had moved away from their traditional reverence for the Church and its teaching.

Although personally religious, Blair steered well clear of religious controversy; his press adviser once told journalists that New Labour did not 'do God'. Blair's belief was in modernity: when the French President Jacques Chirac visited Britain in 2004 to mark a hundred years of the *Entente Cordiale*, Blair took care to show him the modernist architecture of Canary Wharf, the futuristic business centre which had sprung up in London's docklands, rather than the traditional flummery of golden coaches and red-coated guardsmen who usually greeted a foreign head of state. Blair looked forward with eager anticipation to the Millennium, which he intended to mark with an unspecified but breathtaking experience inside a vast Millennium Dome to be built at Greenwich. Despite the build-up, the contents of the Dome proved a damp squib and the Dome itself – outwardly impressive but inwardly empty of ideas or originality – began to look uncomfortably like an image of Blair's New Labour itself. At the New Year celebrations inside the Dome to mark the Millennium, Blair was pictured singing *Auld Lang's Syne* for all he was worth next to a distinctly underwhelmed Queen.

The Queen had good reason to look glum, for the last decade of the twentieth century was one of the most difficult for the

monarchy since the Abdication. In 1992, the fairy-tale royal marriages of her children came crashing to the ground in a series of very public separations and divorces while part of Windsor Castle also went up in flames, leading the Queen to dub the year her 'annus horribilis'. Princess Diana's marital woes were detailed in a widely publicized book, Diana, Her True Story, which she followed up in 1995 with an intimate TV interview in which she claimed that Prince Charles's affair with his old flame, Mrs Camilla Parker Bowles, had made their marriage somewhat crowded; the couple formally divorced the following year. On 31 August 1997, however, Princess Diana was killed in a car crash in Paris and the resulting wave of shock that went through the British people, which saw public weeping and emotion on a scale previously only associated with the peoples of the Mediterranean or Latin America, caught the monarchy completely off-guard. As people piled vast numbers of flowers in front of Buckingham Palace, Tony Blair captured the public mood by calling Diana 'the People's Princess'; that mood soon began to turn ugly when the Queen failed to return to London from Balmoral or to fly a flag at half mast at Buckingham Palace. The monarchy quickly adapted, however, and stage-managed a highly successful funeral with just the right mixture of traditional ceremonial and popular music to satisfy public demand. Slowly but with increasing assurance, the monarchy began to regain public confidence and affection: in 2002 a spectacular open-air party marked the Queen's Golden Jubilee and three years later the Prince of Wales and Mrs Parker Bowles were able to marry with every sign of public sympathy and support. The wedding of Charles and Diana's eldest son, Prince William, to the telegenic but decidedly middle-class Catherine Middleton in 2011 proved hugely popular but was capped by the Queen's own tongue-in-cheek turn for the opening of the London Olympics in 2012, when, to global astonishment, she appeared to parachute into the arena from a helicopter, accompanied by James Bond. It is hard to imagine Queen Victoria having done anything similar, but it was part of the price the monarch was prepared to pay for the institution's survival into the twenty-first century.

Since the early days of the Industrial Revolution the British

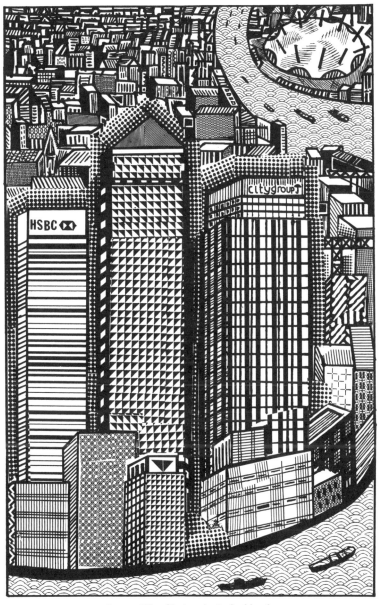

Canary Wharf in London's docklands

A procession celebrated the Golden Jubilee of Queen Elizabeth II

had got used to a breathtaking rate of major social and economic change, but even the age of television, supersonic flight and moon landings was unprepared for the computer revolution that took off in the 1980s. As BBC, Commodore and Spectrum home computers began to appear in the nation's classrooms and round its Christmas trees, entrepreneurs such as the pioneering engineer Clive Sinclair found themselves household names – although his computers proved more successful than his Sinclair C5, an impracticable one-person motorized tricycle that added to the gaiety of the nation but did nothing to resolve chronic overcrowding on the roads. The newly-created office of Mayor of London combined the latest computer technology with a very old idea, the road toll, to produce the Congestion Charge, an attempt to discourage congestion by making motorists pay to drive into the centre of the capital.

Perhaps the most astonishing technological change in every-day life, however, came with the transformation of the humble telephone into a portable, multifunctional computer, able to photograph and film, connect its owner to the Internet, send emails, make payments, present rail or airline tickets or any of a whole host of functions on top of making and receiving phone calls. Having such powerful technology at one's fingertips con-

stituted a veritable social revolution in ways never envisaged by its original inventors. Television programmes were distributed through digital technology, allowing them to be watched, either as a whole or in instalments, at a time and place to suit the convenience of the viewer rather than of the broadcaster – including on mobile phones. Millions connected with each other online via websites known collectively as 'social media', which quickly changed the ways in which ideas were exchanged and spread, with unforeseen implications for how people engaged in political discourse. Canny politicians soon paid as much attention to promoting their policies and personalities online as they ever had to pushing leaflets through domestic letterboxes.

As the world of communications changed, the public grew increasingly impatient with the image of politicians it revealed. To the usual age-old cynicism was added in 2009 an explosive new ingredient when press reports revealed that huge numbers of MPs of all parties, as well as members of the House of Lords, had been twisting the rules covering their expenses to make significant improvements to their standard of living at the taxpayers' expense. Some examples caused as much hilarity as outrage – a Conservative MP's claim for a floating duck house was a case in point – but more serious was the damage done to the integrity of Parliament itself, which was already reeling from a series of scandals involv-

ing the improper payment of money to MPs in return for raising parliamentary questions or for privileged access to ministers, as well as for honours and peerages. Not since the days before the Great Reform Act of 1832 had the parliamentary system appeared so riddled with personal corruption. An increasingly cynical electorate responded by turning in large numbers to political figures outside the political mainstream: the Scottish National Party, the left wing of the Labour Party and the United Kingdom Independence Party, a fringe party that campaigned against the European Union and foreign immigration and which garnered significant numbers of votes from both the Conservatives and Labour.

No issue, however, not even parliamentary corruption, served to sour the public attitude towards politicians, and especially towards Blair's New Labour project, more than the Middle East wars into which Blair led the country in the 2000s. By the 1980s the stability of the region was threatened by the growth of militant Islamic fundamentalism, spearheaded by the 1979 revolution in Iran, which established an angrily anti-Western theocracy led by the Ayatollah Ruhollah Khomeini. In 1989 Khomeini issued a *fatwa* (death sentence) against the British writer Salman Rushdie, whose satirical novel *The Satanic Verses* had provoked outrage in Britain's largely Asian Muslim population, amongst whom the *fatwa* enjoyed levels of support that surprised many British people. Western leaders generally preferred Iran's deadly rival, Iraq, turning a blind eye to the murderous dictatorship of its leader, Saddam Hussein, until in 1990 Saddam launched an invasion of his oil-rich neighbour, Kuwait, prompting a US-led coalition, in which Britain played an important supporting role, to launch a successful counterinvasion.

Ever since Churchill's warm wartime rapport with Roosevelt, British Prime Ministers had sought to establish a close 'special relationship' with American Presidents. Margaret Thatcher had achieved it with Ronald Reagan and Tony Blair with the similarly liberal-minded Bill Clinton. After the Islamic terrorist group al-Qaeda launched its attacks on New York and Washington, DC, on 11 September 2001, Blair immediately offered his support to President George W. Bush, sending British troops to join the US-led invasion of al-Qaeda's support base in Afghanistan. Like Britain's

The MPs' expenses scandal was revealed in the press

previous Afghan adventures, this invasion began successfully but quickly degenerated into a long, drawn-out counter-insurgency campaign against a ruthless guerrilla force operating on its own ground. Even more controversial was the invasion of Iraq ordered by President Bush in 2003 and enthusiastically supported by Tony Blair in the face of enormous and vociferous public opposition. The official reason for the invasion was the supposed ability of the Iraqi regime to launch 'weapons of mass destruction' against the West; when it transpired that the weapons had not existed and that the evidence for them presented to Parliament had been misleading, public anger ran deep. As post-invasion Iraq sank into chaotic infighting and a long drawn-out insurgency, to those on the left Blair's Labour credentials seemed as tarnished as those of Ramsay MacDonald before him.

British troops remained in Iraq until 2011 and in Afghanistan until 2014; but long before then the conflict had taken on sinister overtones much closer to home. On 7 July 2005 a group of British Muslims set off a series of explosions on the London transport network, killing fifty-two people and injuring hundreds more. The terrorists saw their action as part of a global war which they believed Western governments were waging against Muslims in the Middle East and elsewhere. When a violent and ruthless Islamist group calling itself 'Islamic State' emerged amid the chaos of

postwar Iraq and of civil-war torn Syria, many British Muslims, often influenced by messages propagated on social media, travelled to the Middle East to join it. By the 2010s, home-grown Islamist terrorism was one of the most serious security problems facing the country.

Meanwhile, much of the economic optimism of the Blair years had disappeared in the wake of two financial collapses, the first at the turn of the millennium among the fashionable 'dotcom' Internet companies and the second a global banking crisis in 2008, prompted by reckless overinvestment in poor-quality housing by American financiers, which badly affected the economic fortunes of Tony Blair's successor as Prime Minister, Gordon Brown, and contributed to his defeat in the 2010 general election. That election produced a hung parliament for the first time since 1974, allowing the youthful Conservative leader, David Cameron, to wrong-foot his Labour opponents by negotiating a coalition agreement with the Liberal Democrats, granting them a proportion of ministerial positions, including the deputy prime ministership. In office for the first time since Churchill's wartime coalition, the Liberal Democrats found the transition to power difficult; they lost much of their popularity with the young by backing the introduction of tuition fees for university students, a policy they had previously promised to oppose. They also saw their cherished dream of proportional representation disappear when it was decisively rejected in a referendum in 2011. The Liberal Democrats could justly claim to have moderated the government's zeal, but they had long been a haven for political idealists, so they paid a heavy price for the compromises and equivocation that are the necessary accompaniment to political power. In the 2015 election they were reduced to an irrelevant rump and the Conservatives were returned to power on their own, with a small but workable majority.

The 2015 election was also remarkable for the collapse of Labour in its traditional stronghold of Scotland, where all but three parliamentary seats were won by the resurgent Scottish National Party. Since the 1707 Act and Treaty of Union, Scotland had seemed a settled and prosperous partner in the United Kingdom. Glasgow was a major manufacturing and trading centre within the worldwide British Empire, in which many Scots were enthusiastic parti-

Tony Blair addressed troops in Basra, Iraq, in 2004

cipants, and by the late twentieth century the ancient heritage of Anglo-Scottish hostility seemed to have been reduced to a sharper than normal rivalry on the sports field. However, Scots resented the way in which Mrs Thatcher had trialled her unpopular poll tax on them before introducing it in the rest of the United Kingdom. John Major sought to appease the nationalist feeling that was clearly bestirring itself north of the border by the symbolic return to Edinburgh of the ancient Stone of Scone, originally taken to England by King Edward I. In 1997 Scots voted by a large majority for the restoration of a Scottish Parliament at Holyrood, which duly opened in 1999; the Welsh backed the creation of a more limited Welsh Assembly by a smaller margin. Coupled with the Northern Irish Assembly, this meant that more power had been devolved from London than at any time since the eighteenth century. The revival of Scottish and Welsh nationalism prompted an English reaction: the flag of Saint George began to be flown at sporting fixtures and there were even calls in some quarters for greater devolution to the English regions. The scandals of the 2000s over MPs expenses did much to dent the moral authority of the

Westminster Parliament; the Scottish Nationalists increasingly presented Holyrood as the seat of Scotland's 'real' government. In 2014, by agreement between London and Edinburgh, Scotland staged a referendum on independence; although it was rejected by a majority of 55 per cent, support for separation had reached levels previously undreamt of and the vote to remain in the United Kingdom was secured on a promise of still further devolution of power to Holyrood. Barely fifteen years into the new millennium, the future of the United Kingdom itself was looking decidedly uncertain.

In 2011 serious rioting broke out in London and a number of other cities across England. The violence was sparked by the shooting dead by police of a young black man in north London, but these were not race riots: they involved people from many different backgrounds and were fuelled by a range of factors, from social protest to simple theft – the whole incident was strangely reminiscent of the eighteenth-century Gordon Riots. The following year, the London Olympics gave the British an opportunity to reflect before a global audience on the sort of country they believed they had become. In the opening ceremony a living tableau of traditional rural England was violently ripped apart as the factories and towering chimneys of the Industrial Revolution sprang up in its place while the Olympic rings descended into the stadium like molten steel from a Bessemer converter. A procession of Suffragettes, Windrush-generation immigrants and sixties flower people followed each other in a decidedly revisionist narrative pageant of the making of modern Britain. Special attention was given to those gifts to the world of which the twentieth-first century British felt particularly proud: pop music, the National Health Service, the World Wide Web and a flourishing tradition of imaginative literature for children, from *Alice in Wonderland* to *Harry Potter*. It all offered a striking contrast with the industrial pride and imperial confidence of Prince Albert's Great Exhibition of 1851 or the post-war morale-boosting exercise of the 1951 Festival of Britain: Britain had finally emerged from its postwar confusion and regained its self-confidence, though not perhaps in a manner the Victorians – or even Mrs Thatcher – would have recognized.

**Artists Paul Cummins and Tom Piper filled the
Tower of London moat with ceramic poppies**

Reflections on history played a similar role in 2014 as Britain marked the centenary of the First World War. Much of the commemoration focused on the war dead: in a particularly striking installation, the moat of the Tower of London was gradually filled with ceramic poppies, one for each of the British dead of the Great War. But the commemorations also reflected on the role of Empire troops, from India, Africa or the West Indies, and public debate considered the reasons that had led Britain to enter the war a century earlier. Even in the post-modernist new millennium, the British were reflecting on how they had been shaped by their history.

It is fortunately not required of historians that they should be prophets, only that by explaining the past they may provide lessons for the future, since history takes its revenge upon those who ignore it. At least some knowledge of the outlines of England's history and achievements may lead us to hope that, for all the applications of modern society, the English are even now, as Milton suggested they were over 300 years ago, 'not beneath the reach of any point that human capacity can soar to'.

Anglo-Saxon Kings

Up to c.800 the most important kings only are listed; from the reign of Egbert onwards a succession emerges of kings who are effectively rulers of the whole of England

Aelle, King of Sussex (? late 5th century)

Ceawlin, King of Wessex (560–91/2)

Aerhelbert, King of Kent (560–616)

Redwald, King of East Anglia (?–616/27)

Edwin, King of Northumbria (616–33)

Oswald, King of Northumbria (634–42)

Oswy, King of Northumbria (642–70)

Egfrith, King of Northumbria (667–85)

Pendu, King of Mercia (? 632–55)

Wulfhere, King of Mercia (658–674)

Aethelred, King of Mercia (674–704)

Caedwalla, King of Wessex (685–8)

Ine, King of Wessex (688–726)

Wihtred, King of Kent (692–725)

Cenred, King of Mercia (704–9)

Ceolred, King of Mercia (709–16)

Aerhelbald, King of Mercia (716–57)

Ceolwulf, King of Northumbria (729–37)

Aethred, King of Northumbria (774–6, 790–6)

Offa, King of Mercia (757–96)

Beohtric, King of Wessex (786–802)

Conwulf, King of Mercia (796–821)

Egbert (802–39), King of the West Saxons

Ethelwulf (839–55), son of Egbert, King of the West Saxons and Kentishmen

Ethelbald (855–60), son of Ethelwulf, King of the West Saxons

Ethelbert (860–6), son of Ethelwulf, King of the West Saxons and Kentishmen

Ethelred I (866–71), son of Ethelwulf, King of the West Saxons and Kentishmen

Alfred the Great (871–99), son of Ethelwulf, King of the West Saxons

Edward the Elder (899–924), son of Alfred, King of the Angles and Saxons

Athelstan (924–40), son of Edward, King of the West Saxons and Mercians

Edmund (940–6), son of Edward, King of the English

Edred (946–55), Son of Edward, King of the English

Edwy (955–9), son of Edmund, King of the English

Edgar (959–75), son of Edmund, King of the English

Edward the Martyr (975–9), son of Edgar, King of the English

Ethelred II, the Unready (979–1016), son of Edgar, King of England

Edmund Ironside (1016), son of Ethelred, King of England

House of the Skjöldings, or of Denmark

Canute (1016–35), King of the English, Danes and Norwegians

Harthacanute and Harold I, Harefoot (1035), sons of Canute, Kings of Denmark and England

Harold I, Harefoot alone (1035–40)

Harthacanute again (1040–2)

Edward the Confessor (1042–66), son of Ethelred, King of England

Harold II Godwinson (1066), King of England

Normans and Plantagenets 1066–1485

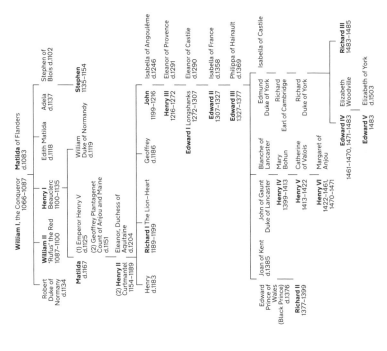

The House of Tudor

Stuarts and Hanoverians 1603-1839

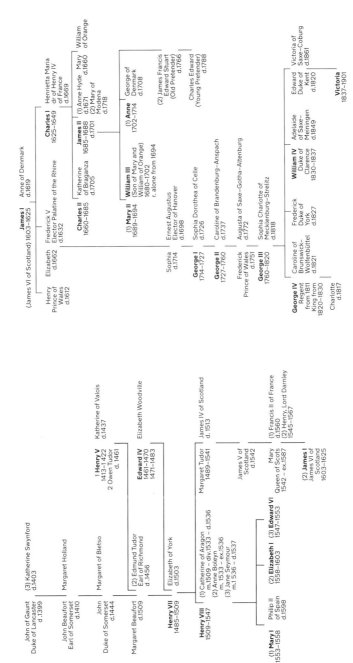

Descendants of Queen Victoria

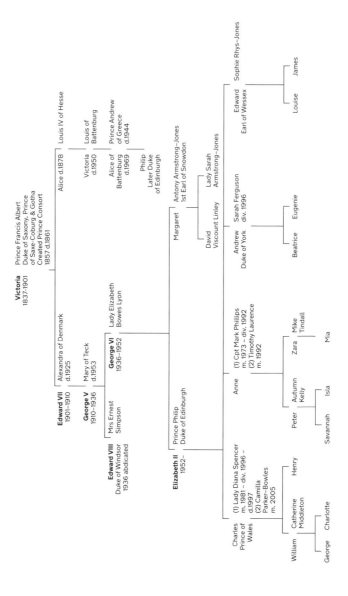

Cathedrals and Country Houses

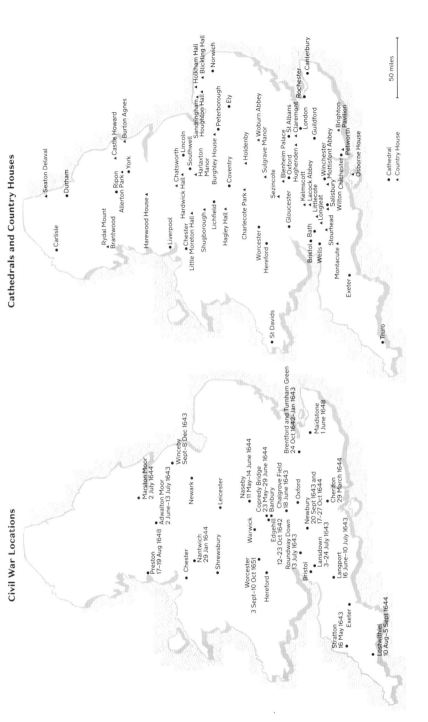

Seaton Delaval ▲
Carlisle •
Durham •
Rydal Mount •
Brantwood •
Ripon •
Castle Howard ▲
Burton Agnes ▲
Allerton Park ▲
York •
Holkham Hall ▲
Blickling Hall ▲
Norwich •
Chatsworth ▲
Lincoln •
Southwell •
Sandringham ▲
Harlaxton Manor ▲
Houghton Hall ▲
Peterborough •
Ely •
Woburn Abbey ▲
Hardwick Hall ▲
Chester •
Little Moreton Hall ▲
Shugborough •
Lichfield •
Hagley Hall ▲
Coventry •
Charlecote Park •
Holdenby ▲
Sulgrave Manor ▲
Harewood House ▲
Liverpool •
Sezincote •
Blenheim Palace ▲
St Albans •
Oxford •
Hughenden ▲
Claremont ▲
Canterbury •
Rochester •
London •
Brighton Pavilion •
Guildford •
Petworth House ▲
Worcester •
Hereford •
Gloucester •
Kelmscott •
Lacock Abbey ▲
Bath •
Littlecote ▲
Bristol •
Longleat ▲
Wells •
Stourhead ▲
Salisbury •
Winchester •
Wilton Chichester • Mottisfont Abbey ▲
Montacute ▲
Osborne House ▲
Exeter •
St Davids •
Truro •
• Cathedral
▲ Country House
50 miles

Civil War Locations

Marston Moor
2 July 1644
Adwalton Moor
2 June 1644
Winceby
Sept–8 Dec 1643
Preston
17–19 Aug 1648
Newark •
Leicester •
Chester •
Nantwich
29 Jan 1644
Naseby
11 May–14 June 1644
Copredy Bridge
23 May–29 June 1644
Banbury
Chalgrove Field
18 June 1643
Brentford and Turnham Green
24 Oct 1642–Jan 1643
Maidstone
1 June 1648
Warwick •
Edgehill
12–23 Oct 1642
Roundway Down
13 July 1643
Oxford •
Newbury
20 Sept 1643 and
17–27 Oct 1644
Cheriton
29 March 1644
Worcester
3 Sept–10 Oct 1651
Shrewsbury •
Hereford •
Lansdown
3–24 July 1643
Bristol •
Langport
16 June–10 July 1643
Stratton
16 May 1643
Exeter •
Lostwithiel
10 Aug–5 Sept 1644

237

Map of England

Lindisfarne (Holy Island)

Berwick-upon-Tweed

Bamburgh

Alnwick

Hadrian's Wall

Newcastle upon Tyne

Carlisle

Durham

Darlington

Whitby

Scarborough

Richmond

Rievaulx

Jervaulx

Ripon

York

Beverley

Kingston upon Hull

Grimsby

Leeds (Kirkstall Abbey)

Doncaster

Fountains

Harrogate

Wakefield

Grasmere

Kendal

Bradford

Sheffield

Blackpool

Preston

Blackstone Edge

Manchester

Liverpool

Anglesey

Hartlech

Llangollen

Shrewsbury •
Ironbridge •

Ludlow •

Hereford •

Brecon •

Cardigan

Carmarthen •

Pembroke •

Swansea •

Caerphilly •
Cardiff •

Chepstow •

Berkeley •

Gloucester •

Cheltenham •

Worcester •

Dudley •

Coventry •
Kenilworth •
Warwick •

Birmingham •

Brixworth •
Northampton •

Stratford-on-Avon •

Evesham •

Chedworth •

Cirencester •

Woodstock •
Oxford •
Abingdon •

Banbury •

Aylesbury •

St Albans •

Chelmsford •

Bedford •

Cambridge •

Earl's Barton •

Bury St Edmunds •

Long Melford •
Lavenham •

Little Wenham •

Colchester •

Ipswich •
Aldeburgh •
Framlingham •

Thetford •

Ely •

Peterborough •
Fotheringhay •

Oakham •

Rockingham •

Leicester •
Bradgate Park •

King's Lynn •

Great Yarmouth
Norwich •

Canterbury •
Faversham •
Isle of Sheppey
Dover •
Folkstone •

Rochester •
Maidstone •

Battle •
Hastings •

Herstmonceux •
Lewes •
Arundel • Brighton •
Chichester •
Fishbourne •

Tunbridge Wells •

Guildford •

Greenwich •
London •
Eton •

Windsor •
Reading •
Windmill Hill •
Newbury •
West Kennett •

Silchester •

Basingstoke •
Steeple Ashton •

Stonehenge •

Avebury •
Devizes •

Bath •
Bradford-on-Avon •

Bristol •

Wells •

Glastonbury •

Huish Episcopi •
Cadbury Castle •

Yeovil •

Taunton •

Barnstaple •

Exeter •

Launceston •

Plymouth •

Wadebridge •

Tintagel •

Truro •

Penzance •

Salisbury •

Winchester •
Netley •
Southampton •

Portsmouth •
Isle of Wight

Bournemouth •

Dorchester •
Maiden Castle •

Chichester •

30 miles

Central London west of Piccadilly

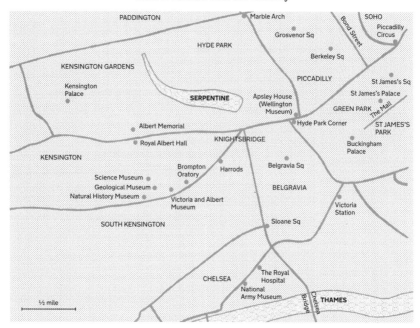

PADDINGTON

Marble Arch

SOHO

Grosvenor Sq

Piccadilly Circus

HYDE PARK

Berkeley Sq

KENSINGTON GARDENS

PICCADILLY

St James's Sq

Kensington Palace

SERPENTINE

Apsley House (Wellington Museum)

St James's Palace

GREEN PARK

The Mall

Albert Memorial

Hyde Park Corner

ST JAMES'S PARK

Royal Albert Hall

KNIGHTSBRIDGE

Buckingham Palace

KENSINGTON

Brompton Oratory

Harrods

Belgravia Sq

Science Museum

BELGRAVIA

Geological Museum

Natural History Museum

Victoria and Albert Museum

Victoria Station

SOUTH KENSINGTON

Sloane Sq

CHELSEA

The Royal Hospital

National Army Museum

THAMES

Chelsea Bridge

½ mile

Central London east of Piccadilly

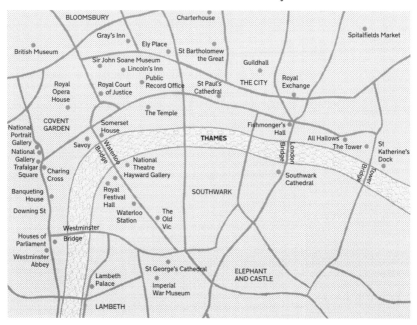

BLOOMSBURY

Charterhouse

Spitalfields Market

Gray's Inn

Ely Place

St Bartholomew the Great

British Museum

Sir John Soane Museum

Guildhall

Lincoln's Inn

Public Record Office

St Paul's Cathedral

THE CITY

Royal Exchange

Royal Opera House

Royal Court of Justice

COVENT GARDEN

The Temple

National Portrait Gallery

Somerset House

Fishmonger's Hall

All Hallows

The Tower

St Katherine's Dock

Savoy

THAMES

National Gallery

Waterloo Bridge

London Bridge

Trafalgar Square

Charing Cross

National Theatre Hayward Gallery

Southwark Cathedral

Tower Bridge

Banqueting House

Royal Festival Hall

SOUTHWARK

Downing St

Waterloo Station

The Old Vic

Westminster Bridge

Houses of Parliament

ELEPHANT AND CASTLE

Westminster Abbey

St George's Cathedral

Lambeth Palace

Imperial War Museum

LAMBETH

Chronological Charts

World Chronology

British Chronology

World Chronology		British Chronology	
		c5000 BC–2500 BC	Neolithic Britain
2660 BC	First pyramid built		
c2500 BC	Menhir statues of Sardinia and Southern France	c3250 BC	West Kennet Long Barrow built
2330–2180 BC	6th Egyptian dynasty	c2500 BC–1600 BC	Early and Middle Bronze Ages
1972 BC	Hammurabi accedes to the throne in Babylon	c2200 BC–1300 BC	Stonehenge built
c1750 BC	Hammurabi's 'Eye for an Eye' law code	2000 BC–1600 BC	Avebury Stones erected
c1595 BC	Hittites take Babylon		
c1400 BC	Destruction of Knossos	c2000 BC	Immigration of Beaker Folk
c1290 BC	The Temple of Abu Simbel begun	c1600 BC–AD 43	Iron Age
c1250 BC	Agamemnon, King of Mycenae, leads Greeks against Troy		
c970 BC	Death of Solomon, King of Israel	c1000 BC	First hill forts built
		c800 BC	Immigration of Celts
776 BC	First Olympic Games		
753 BC	Traditional date of founding of Rome by Romulus and Remus		
594 BC	Solon Archon at Athens		
558–529 BC	Cyrus the Great ruler of the Persian Empire		
490 BC	Greeks defeat Persians at Marathon		
c479 BC	Death of Confucius		
430–404 BC	Peloponnesian War between Athens and Sparta		
399 BC	Trial of Socrates		
347 BC	Death of Plato		
323 BC	Death of Alexander the Great		
322 BC	Death of Aristotle		
264 BC	Beginning of Punic Wars between Rome and Carthage		
218 BC	Hannibal crosses the Alps		
c214 BC	Great Wall of China finished		
206 BC–AD 200	Han dynasty in China		
		100 BC	Immigration of Belgae
59 BC	Julius Caesar appointed Consul	55 BC	Julius Caesar's first expedition to Britain
		50 BC	Cassivellaunus, British chieftain
44 BC	Caesar assassinated	AD 43	Roman invasion
27 BC–AD 30	Octavian (Augustus) first Roman AD 14 Emperor		
AD 30	Jesus of Nazareth condemned to death	49	Foundation of Colchester
		c50	Foundation of London
		51	King Caractacus defeated
		61	Rebellion of Iceni under Boudicca
64	Rome burned in time of Nero and Christians persecuted	70–84	Conquest of Wales and north
70	Destruction of the Temple in Jerusalem	c75	Fishbourne Palace built
79	Destruction of Pompeii and Herculaneum by eruption of Vesuvius	78–c85	Agricola Governor of Britain
105	Chinese invent paper		
110–11	Juvenal's satires		
111–14	Trajan's Forum built		
117–38	Reign of Hadrian	122	Hadrian's Wall begun
124	Pantheon built at Rome		
135	Capture of Jerusalem	c140	Theatre built at Verulamium (St Albans)
161–80	Reign of Marcus Aurelius	c143	Antonine Wall in Scotland begun
		185	Antonine Wall abandoned
		195–7	Usurper emperor Albinus in Britain
		197	Barbarians overrun Hadrian's Wall
216	Baths of Caracalla built in Rome	c208	Hadrian's Wall rebuilt by Septimius Severus

World Chronology		British Chronology		Art, Architecture & Literature in England	
284–305	Reign of Diocletian	287–296	Carausius and Allectus usurp emperors in Britain		
306–37	Reign of Constantine	306	Constantine the Great proclaimed Emperor at York		
330	Constantine founds new city Constantinople				
376	Visigoths cross Danube	407	Constantine the Third proclaimed Emperor in Britain		
		409	Last Roman legions leave		
410	Visigoths sack Rome	c450	Contact between Rome and Britain severed		
450	Metal stirrup in use in Asian steppes				
453	Death of Attila the Hun	c450	Hengist and Horsa settle in Kent		
455	Vandals sack Rome	c455	Hengist rebels against Vortigern		
469	Visigoths begin conquest of Spain	c470	Saxons settle in Sussex		
		c495	Saxons settle in Wessex		
511	Death of Clovis, King of the Franks	c510	Battle of Mount Badon		
529	Benedictine Order founded				
537	Haghia Sophia finished in Constantinople	597	Arrival of Augustine		
619–906	Tang dynasty in China				
625	Mohammed begins dictating Koran	664	Synod of Whitby		
		668	Arrival of Archbishop Theodore		
		672	Synod of Hertford		
674	Arabs attack Constantinople	c672	Rise of Mercia		
711	Arabs land in Spain	c698	Lindisfarne Gospels		
751	Earliest printed book, Buddhist Diamond Sutra	735	Death of Bede		
788	Great Mosque at Cordoba begun	757	Offa becomes King of Mercia		
800	Charlemagne crowned Emperor of West	c793	First Viking raids on Britain		
		c800	Beowulf, Old English epic poem		
860	Russians besiege Constantinople	829	Northumbrians submit to Egbert, King of West Saxons		
c870	Invention of gunpowder in China	867	Northumbria falls to Danes		
		871	Accession of King Alfred		
		878	Alfred defeats Danes		
880	Foundation of Kiev	886	Danelaw established in Northern England		
885	Normans besiege Paris				
889	Angkor founded	c891	Anglo-Saxon Chronicle begun		
910	Foundation of Benedictine Abbey at Cluny				
911	Rollo the Viking becomes first Duke of Normandy				
933	Foundation of Delhi	960	St Dunstan becomes Archbishop of Canterbury		
962	Otto I crowned Holy Roman Emperor	973	Edgar acknowledged as their overlord by British princes		
987	Accession of Hugh Capet in France	991	Danegeld first levied		
992	First commercial treaty between Venice and Byzantium	1016	Cnut chosen as King		
1035	William the Bastard becomes Duke of Normandy	1042	Edward the Confessor becomes King		
1055	Seljuk Turks at Baghdad	1065	Westminster Abbey consecrated		
		1066	Battle of Hastings		
		1066	William I crowned in Westminster Abbey	c1070	Windsor Castle begun
1071	Jerusalem captured by Seljuk Turks	1071	Hereward the Wake holds Isle of Ely against William	1070	Canterbury Cathedral begun
c1075	Bayeux Tapestry			1078–88	Tower of London built
1075–1122	Santiago de Compostela built				
1076	Normans take Salerno				
1085	Toledo taken from Moors	1086	Domesday survey	1093	Rib vaulting in Durham Cathedral aisles

1088 Chinese astronomical water clock

1096–99 First Crusade

c1100 *Chanson de Roland*, earliest *chanson de geste*

1115 St Bernard founds Abbey of Clairvaux

1116 Bologna University founded

1118 Knights Templar founded

1130 Cluny Abbey completed

1135 First use of flying buttress in France

1137–44 Abbey of Saint-Denis, Paris

1138 Arabic numerals in use in West

1147–9 Second Crusade

1163 Notre Dame, Paris begun

1174 Saladin Sultan of Egypt

1187 Saladin takes Jerusalem

1190 Mariner's compass in use in West

1190 Military order of Teutonic Knights founded

1190 Third Crusade begins

1192 Yoromito Minamoto becomes Shogun, hereditary military dictator in Japan

1194–1260 Chartres Cathedral built

1200 University of Paris granted Charter

1201 Fourth Crusade begins

1204 Crusaders attack Constantinople

1208–13 Albigensian Crusade

1210 Genghis Khan invades China

1210 St Francis of Assissi founds Franciscan Order of Friars

1212 Children's Crusade

1215 Dominican Order of Friars founded

1215 Fourth Lateran Council

1222 University of Padua founded

1224 Mongols under Ghenghis Khan invade Eastern Europe

1232 Chinese use rockets in warfare

1234 Mongols overthrow Ch'in dynasty

c1236 *Roman de la Rose*, French epic of courtly love

1240 Mongols conquer south Russia

1248 Ferdinand of Castile takes Seville from Moors

1260 Kublai Khan emperor of Mongolia

1267–73 Thomas Aquinas's *Summa Theologiae*

1276 Kublai Khan takes Hangzhou

1283 Cimabue's Cricifix, S. Croce, Florence

1087 Accession of William II

1093 Anselm becomes Archbishop

1095 Death of St Wulfstan

1100 Accession of Henry I

1128 Marriage of Empress Matilda to Geoffrey of Anjou

1135 Accession of Stephen

1139 Canonization of Edward the Confessor

1139–53 Civil war

1141 Stephen captured

1152 Henry of Anjou (Henry II) marries Eleanor of Aquitaine

1153 Henry of Anjou invades England

1154 Accession of Henry II

1162 Thomas Becket Archbishop of Canterbury

1170 Becket murdered

1173 William the Lion, King of Scotland invades north of England; Becket canonized

1189 Accession of Richard I

1193 Richard I imprisoned in Germany

1193 Hubert Walter Archbishop of Canterbury

1195 Office of Justice of the Peace

1195–0 Richard I engaged in warfare in France

1199 Accession of King John

1207 Stephen Langton Archbishop of Canterbury

1208–14 England placed under interdict by Pope

1209 King John excommunicated

1214 At battle of Bouvines King Philip II Augustus of France defeats King John in alliance with emperor Otto IV and Count of Flanders

1215 Civil war in England; King John obliged to sign Magna Carta

1216 French army lands in Kent

1216 Accession of Henry III

1221–4 Dominicans and Franciscans arrive in England

1240 Death of Llewellyn I ap Gruffyd

1258 Barons assume royal government: Provisions of Oxford

1259 Treaty of Paris between France and England

1264 Battle of Lewes: Henry III captured

1265 Battle of Evesham

1272 Accession of Edward I

1282 Death of Llewellyn II ap Gruffyd

1282–3 Edward's conquest of Wales

1097 Westminster Hall begun

1121–54 *Peterborough Chronicle*: includes annals up to death of King Stephen

1123 St Bartholomew's Hospital, London founded

1125 William of Malmesbury's ecclesiastical history *Gesta Pontificum Anglorum*

1131–2 Tintern, Rievaulx and Fountains Abbeys founded

1133 First St Bartholomew's Fair

1154 Geoffrey of Monmouth's *History of the Kings of Britain*

c1154 York Minster begun

1165–79 Windsor Castle rebuilt in stone

c1175 Wells Cathedral begun

1180 Sternpost rudders in use

1181–7 Keep of Dover Castle built

1185 First windmill recorded

1195 Lichfield Cathedral begun

1209 London Bridge finished in stone

1220 Salisbury Cathedral begun

c1223 Robert Grosseteste Chancellor of Oxford

1235 Royal menagerie opened in Tower of London

1236 Matthew Paris succeeds Roger of Wendover as chronicler at St Alban's Monastery

1247 Bethlehem Royal Hospital (later Bedlam lunatic asylum) opened

1249 University College, Oxford founded

1267–8 Roger Bacon's *Opus Maius*, a summary of current scientific knowledge

1275 London's Custom House build on Old West Quay

1281 Peterhouse, Cambridge founded

World Chronology	British Chronology	Art, Architecture and Literature
1291 Acre captured by Mamluks	1290 Jews expelled from England	1296 Edward I takes Stone of Scone to Westminster
	1295 Meeting of Model Parliament	
c1300 Earliest manufacture of gunpowder in West	1296 Edward invades Scotland	
	1306 Rebellion of Robert Bruce	
1306 Jews expelled from France	1307 Accession of Edward II	
1309 Papacy moves to Avignon		
1310 Knights of St John take Rhodes	1314 Battle of Bannockburn	
1311 Duccio completes altarpiece for Siena Cathedral		1326 Oriel College, Oxford, founded
1321 Death of Dante Alighieri	1321–2 Civil war	
c1325 Rise of Aztecs in Mexico	1327 Accession of Edward III	
1334 Giotto begins work on Florence campanile	1337 Start of Hundred Years' War	1337 Edward II's tomb, Gloucester Cathedral, begun
		1347 Pembroke College, Cambridge, founded
1345 Ponte Vecchio, Florence completed	1340 Battle of Sluys	
	1346 Battles of Crécy and Neville's Cross	1348 Foundation of the Order of the Garter
1349–51 Boccaccio's *Decameron*	1347 Calais captured	c1350 *Sir Gawain and the Green Knight*
	1348 Black Death	
		c1362 Langland's *Vision of Piers Ploughman*
1356 Ottoman Turks invade Europe	1356 Battle of Poitiers	
1368–1644 Ming dynasty in China	1370 Black Prince sacks Limoges	
	1376 Death of Black Prince	1379 New College, Oxford, founded
1377 Papacy returns to Rome	1377 Accession of Richard II	1380 Wyclif translates Bible
1378 Beginning of Great Schism		1386 Salisbury Cathedral clock
	1381 Peasants' Revolt	1387 William of Wykeham founds Winchester College
		1387–1400 Chaucer's *Canterbury Tales*
		1390 John Gower's *Confessio Amantis*
	1399 Accession of Henry IV	1392 Wells Cathedral Clock
	1400 Rebellion of Owain Glyndwr	c1400 The Wilton Diptych
1402 Ghiberti begins work on doors of Florentine Baptistery		
1404 Venice acquires Verona and Vicenza	1413 Accession of Henry V	
1408–9 Donatello's *David*	1415 Battle of Agincourt	
1415–17 Council of Constance ends Great Schism		c1420 Fan vaulting at Gloucester Cathedral
1418 Brunelleschi chosen to build dome of Florence Cathedral	1420 Treaty of Troyes	
	1420 Henry V marries Catherine of Valois	1422–1529 Paston family letters
	1422 Accession of Henry VI	1422 Earliest records of Lincoln's Inn
1426–8 Masaccio frescoes, Brancacci Chapel, Florence	1430 Joan of Arc burned	
1434 Van Eyck's *Betrothal of the Arnolfini*	1436 English evacuate Paris	1440 Eton College founded
1434 Cosimo de' Medici becomes ruler of Florence		
1440 Fra Angelico's *Annunciation*, S. Marco, Florence		
1442 Diaz reaches mouth of the Senegal River	1445 Henry VI marries Margaret of Anjou	1446 King's College Chapel, Cambridge, begun
	1453 End of Hundred Years' War	
1450 Uccello's *Battle of San Romano*		
1453 Constantinople falls to the Turks	1455 Outbreak of the Wars of the Roses	
1454 Gutenberg uses movable type	1459 Defeat of the Duke of York	
1454 Peace of Lodi	1461 Accession of Edward IV	
	1471 Edward IV defeats Earl of Warwick at Tewkesbury	1469–70 Malory's *Le Morte d'Arthur*
	1471 Death of Henry VI	
		1473 St Catherine's College, Cambridge, founded
		1474 William Caxton prints first book in English

1477 Botticelli's *Primavera*		
1480 Ivan IV defeats Golden Horde		1478 St George's Chapel, Windsor, founded
1482 Torquemada appointed Inquisitor General		
	1483 Death of Edward IV; accession of Richard III	
	1485 Battle of Bosworth Field	
	1485 Accession of Henry VII	
1487 Diaz rounds Cape of Good Hope	1487 Rebellion of Lambert Simnel	
1492 Fall of Granada		
1492 Christopher Columbus lands in West Indies		
1495 Leonardo's *Last Supper*		
1498 Vasco da Gama lands at Calicut, India		
1498 Savonarola executed	1499 John Cabot discovers Newfoundland	
1503–7 Leonardo's *Mona Lisa*		
1508 Michelangelo begins ceiling of Sistine Chapel		
1509 Erasmus's *In praise of Folly*	1509 Accession of Henry VIII	1510 John Colet founds St Paul's School
	1513 Battle of Flodden	1514 Hampton Court Palace begun
1516 Macchiavelli's *The Prince*	1515 Wolsey appointed Lord Chancellor	1516 More's *Utopia*
1517 Luther's 95 Theses published		1519 Henry VII's Chapel, Westminster Abbey, completed
1518 Titian's *The Assumption*		
1521 Fall of Aztec Empire		
1521 Diet of Worms signals beginning of Reformation		
1527 Sack of Rome		
1529 Turks besiege Vienna	1529 Peace of Cambrai	
1533 Fall of Inca Empire	1533 Henry VIII marries Anne Boleyn	1536 Holbein's *Henry VIII*
1534 Foundation of Society of Jesus	1534 Act of Supremacy	
1535 Cartier discovers St Lawrence River	1535 More and Fisher executed	
1536 Calvin goes to Geneva	1536–40 Dissolution of the Monasteries	
1543 Copernicus's *De Revolutionibus*	1547 Accession of Edward VI	1546 Christ Church, Oxford, founded
	1549 First Book of Common Prayer	
1553 Tobacco introduced into Europe	1553 Accession of Mary	1555 Trinity and St John's Colleges, Oxford, founded
	1554 Wyatt's rebellion	
	1558 Accession of Elizabeth I	
	1559 Peace of Cateau–Cambrésis	1563 Foxe's *Book of Martyrs*
	1568 Mary Stuart arrives in England	
1570 Palldio's *Quattre Libri dcll'Architottura*	1569 Rebellion of the northern earls	1570 Royal Exchange opened
1571 Battle Lepanto	1570 Elizabeth I excommunicated	1572 Byrd and Tallis organists at Chapel Royal
1572 St Bartholomew's Day Massacre		
1584 Sir Walter Ralegh founds Virginia	1587 Mary Stuart executed	1587 Rose Theatre opened
1586 El Greco's *Burial of Count Orgaz*	1588 Spanish Armada	1589 Hakluyt's *Voyages*
1589 Henry III of France murdered		1590 Sidney's *Arcadia*
1594 Henry IV enters Paris		1590–6 Spenser's *Faerie queene*
1598 Edict of Nantes, granting tolerance to French Protestants		1590 Marlowe's *Tamburlaine the Great*
		c1590 Shakespeare's *Henry VI*
		c1594 Shakespeare's *Romeo and Juliet*
		c1598 Shakespeare's *Henry V*
		1598 Ben Johnson's *Every Man in his Humour*
		1599 Globe Theatre completed
	1600 East India Company founded	1600 Gilbert's *De Magnete*
	1601 Essex's rebellion	1601 Shakespeare's *Hamlet*
	1603 Accession of James I	1602 Bodleian Library opened
1605 Cervantes's *Don Quixote*	1605 Gunpowder Plot	1605 Shakespeare's *King Lear* and *Macbeth*
1609 Galileo makes his telescope	1609 Rebellion in Ireland	
	1611 James I's First Parliament dissolved	1611 Authorized Version of the Bible
1618 Defenestration of Prague: beginning of the Thirty Years' War		c1611 Shakespeare's *The Tempest*
		1616 Death of Shakespeare
1619 Slaves imported into Virginia from Africa	1620 Pilgrim Fathers emigrate to New England	1622 Inigo Jones's Banqueting House finished

World Chronology		British Chronology		Art, Architecture and Literature	
1620	Battle of the White Mountain	1624–30	War with Spain	1624	Pembroke College, Oxford, founded
1620	Fran Hals's *Laughing Cavalier*	1625	Accession of Charles I		
1626	Dutch found New Amsterdam (New York)	1626–9	War with France	1628	Harvey explains circulation of blood
1628	Richelieu starves Huguenots into submission at La Rochelle	1628	Petition of Right		
		1629	Parliament dissolved by Charles I		
1631	Sack of Magdeburg			1631–3	St Paul's, Covent Garden, built
1632–53	Shah Jahan builds Taj Mahal			1632	Van Dyck appointed Painter–in–Ordinary to Charles I
1635	Académie Française founded				
1636	Harvard University founded			1633–40	Wilton House built
1637	Corneille's *Le Cid*	1640	Long Parliament called	1640	Queen's House, Greenwich, completed
1640	Spain loses Portugal	1641	Grand Remonstrance		
1641	Dutch take Malacca from Portugal	1642	Attempted arrest of Five Members	1641	John Evelyn begins his diary
1642	Tasmania discovered and the French found Montreal	1642	Outbreak of Civil War	1643	Milton's *Areopagitica* in defence of free speech
1642	Rembrandt's *The Night Watch*	1642	Battle of Edgehill		
1643	Accession of Louis XIV to French throne				
1644	Peking taken over by Manchus and foundation of Ch'ing dynasty	1644	Battle of Marston Moor		
		1645	Battle of Naseby		
1648	Independence of United Provinces recognized at the Hague	1648	Battle of Preston		
		1649	Charles I executed		
1648	End of Thirty Years' War by Peace of Westphalia	1649–50	Cromwell conquers Ireland		
		1650–2	Cromwell conquers Scotland	1651	Hobbe's *Leviathan*
		1651	Battle of Worcester		
		1652	First Anglo–Dutch war		
		1653	Cromwell becomes Lord Protector		
1657	Bernini begins colonnades of St Peter's, Rome	1658	Richard Cromwell succeeds father		
		1659	Richard Cromwell overthrown by army	1660	Dryden's *Astraea Redux*
1661	Louis XIV absolute ruler of France	1660	Restoration of the Monarchy: Accession of Charles II	1660	Royal Society constituted
1664	Ottoman Turks occupy Hungary	1664–5	Great Plague		
1670	Molière's *Bourgeois Gentilhomme*	1666	Great Fire		
		1667	The Dutch in the Medway	1667	Milton's *Paradise Lost*
1670	Hudson's Bay Company founded	1674	End of war against Dutch		
1674	Jan Sobiewski elected King of Poland			1675	Wycherley's *Country Wife*
1677	Racine's *Phèdre*			1678	Bunyan's *Pilgrim's Progress*
1683	Revocation of Edict of Nantes				
		1685	Accession of James II	1687	Newton's *Principia Mathematica*
		1688	Glorious Revolution		
		1689	Accession of William III and Mary II	1694	Bank of England established
		1701	War of Spanish Succession begins		
1703	Peter the Great founds St Petersburg	1702	Accession of Anne		
		1704	Battle of Blenheim	1705	Blenheim Palace begun
		1707	Union of England and Scotland	1710	St Paul's Cathedral completed
1715	Death of Louis XIV; accession of Louis XV to French throne	1714	Accession of George I	1710	Defoe's *Robinson Crusoe*
		1715	Jacobite rebellion		
		1720	South Sea Bubble		
		1727	Accession of George II	1726	Swift's *Gulliver's Travels*
1741	Frederick the Great defeats Austrians			1729	Pope's *Dunciad*
		1742	Fall of Robert Walpole	1742	Handel's *Messiah*
		1745	Jacobite rebellion	1749	Fielding's *Tom Jones*
1755	Lisbon earthquake	1756	Seven Years' War begins	1753	British Museum founded
		1757	Battle of Plessey		
		1759	Quebec captured		
		1760	Accession of George III	1761	Sterne's *Tristam Shandy*
1770	Cook sights Australia	1763	Peace of Paris	1768	Royal Academy founded with Sir Joshua Reynolds as its first President
		1773	Boston Tea Party		

		1769 Watt's steam engine
	1776 American Declaration of Independence	
		1776 Gibbon's *Decline and Fall of the Roman Empire*
	1780 Gordon Riots	
		1776 Smith's *Wealth of Nations*
	1781 Surrender at Yorktown	
	1783 Americans win independence	
	1784 Wesley founds Methodist Church	
1786 Mozart's *Marriage of Figaro*		
1789 French Revolution		
		1796 Vaccination against smallpox
1795 Mungo Park explores Niger		
		1798 Malthus's *Essay on Population*
1796 Bonaparte's Italian Campaign		
	1803 War with France	
1804 Beethoven's *Eroica Symphony*		
	1805 Battle of Trafalgar	
		1805 Wordsworth's *Prelude*
1808 Goethe's *Faust*		
1808–14 Peninsula War		
	1811 Luddite disturbances	
		1813 Austen's *Pride and Prejudice*
1812 Napoleon's retreat from Moscow		
	1815 Battle of Waterloo	
1813 Napoleon defeated at Leipzig		
	1819 Peterloo massacre	
		1819–24 Byron's *Don Juan*
1817 Venezuela independent under Bolivare		
	1820 Accession of George IV	
		1821 Constable's *Hay Wain*
		1824 National Gallery founded
	1825 Trade unions legalized	
		1829 Stephenson's *Rocket*
	1829 Catholic Emancipation	
		1831 Faraday discovers electrical induction
1827 Battle of Navarino		
1830 Revolution in Paris		
		1832 Tennyson's *Lady of Shalott*
	1832 Great Reform Bill	
1832 Greek independence		
	1833 Factory Act	
	1833 Slavery abolished in British Empire	
	1834 Transportation of 'Tolpuddle Martyrs'	
1836 Battle of Alamo		
	1836 Chartist movement launched	
	1837 Accession of Queen Victoria	
		1839 Turner's *Fighting Temeraire*
	1838 Anti-Corn Law League	
		1847 Charlotte Brontë's *Jane Eyre*
	1840 Penny Post	
		1847 Emily Brontë's *Wuthering Heights*
1847 Liberia becomes independent		
	1846 Repeal of Corn Laws	
1848 Communist Manifesto		
		1848 Thackeray's *Vanity Fair*
	1851 Great Exhibition	
		1848 Macaulay's *History of England*
		1848 Mill's *Principles of Political Economy*
1850 Taiping Rebellion		
		1849 Dickens's *David Copperfield*
1851 Verdi's *Rigoletto*		
1851 Melville's *Moby Dick*		
1852 Napoleon III proclaimed Emperor		
	1854 Crimean War	
		1855 Trollope's *The Warden*
	1857 Opium War	
1856 Flaubert's *Madame Bovary*		
	1857 Indian Mutiny	
		1859 Darwin's *Origin of Species*
1860 Garibaldi proclaims Victor Emmanuel King of Italy		
		1860 Barry's *Houses of Parliament* completed
1861–5 American Civil War		
1862 Turgenev's *Fathers and Sons*		
1864 Pasteur invents pasteurization		
1865 Lincoln assassinated		
1869 Suez Canal opened		
	1868 Disraeli becomes Prime Minister	
1870 Franco–Prussian War		
		1871 Royal Albert Hall
	1868 Gladstone's first Liberal government	
		1872 George Eliot's *Middlemarch*
1873 Tolstoy's *Anna Karenina*		
1874 First Impressionist Exhibition		
1876 Bell's telephone		
	1876 Queen Victoria becomes Empress of India	
1876 Wagner's *Ring Cycle* performed		
		1878 Wilde's *Lady Windemere's Fan*
1879 Dostoyevsky's *The Brothers Karamazov*		
	1879 Zulu War	
1879 Edison's electric light		
	1880 First Boer War	
	1882 Occupation of Egypt	
1882 Daimler's petrol engine		
	1885 Gordon killed at Khartoum	
1888 Van Gogh's *Sunflowers*		
	1893 Irish Home Rule Bill rejected by Lords	
		1894 Shaw's *Arms and the Man*
		1895 Henry Wood starts Promenade Concerts
1895 Marconi's wireless		
	1896 Sudan conquered	
		1896 Hardy's *Jude the Obscure*
1898 Curies discover radium		
	1899 Second Boer War	
		1899 Elgar's *Enigma Variations*
1900 Boxer Rebellion		
	1901 Accession of Edward VII	

World Chronology		British Chronology		Art, Architecture and Literature	
1904	Freud's *Psychopathology of Everyday Life*	1904	Anglo–French entente	1904	Conrad's *Nostromo*
1905	Russian–Japanese War				
1905	Einstein's theory of relativity				
1907	Picasso's *Les Demoiselles d'Avignon*	1911	First National Health Insurance Bill	1913	Lawrence's *Sons and Lovers*
1915	D.W. Griffith's *Birth of a Nation*	1914–18	First World War		
1917	USA enters First World War	1916	Battles of Somme and Jutland		
1917	Russian Revolution	1917	Battle of Passchendaele		
		1919	Treaty of Versailles	1921	Rutherford and Chadwick split the atom
1922	Mussolini's March on Rome			1922	Eliot's *The Wasteland*
1924	Death of Lenin: Stalin assumes power in Soviet Union	1924	First Labour government	1922	Joyce's *Ulysses*
1929	Wall Street Crash	1926	General Strike	1926	Baird invents television
		1929	Vote for women over 21	1930	Waugh's *Vile Bodies*
		1931	National government led by Ramsay Macdonald		
		1931	Gold standard abandoned	1932	Broadcasting House built
1933	Hitler becomes Chancellor			1937	Whittle invents jet engine
1937	Picasso's *Guernica*	1938	Chamberlain and Hitler at Munich		
1939	Franco captions Madrid	1939–45	Second World War	1940	Greene's *The Power and The Glory*
		1940	Battle of Britain		
		1940	Churchill becomes Prime Minister		
1941	Welles's *Citizen Kane*	1940	Withdrawal from Dunkirk		
1941	Pearl Harbor	1942	Battle of El Alamein		
1944	Liberation of Paris	1944	D–Day invasion of France	1945	Moore's *Family Group*
1945	Yalta Conference	1945	Labour government under Attlee	1949	Orwell's *1984*
1945	Atomic bomb				
1947	Independence for India, Pakistan, Burma				
1949	People's Republic of China proclaimed				
1949	NATO founded	1951	Festival of Britain	1951	Martin's Royal Festival Hall
1950	Outbreak of Korean War			1953	Bacon's *Study after Velasquez's Portrait of Pope Innocent X*
1953	Death of Stalin			1954	Amis's *Lucky Jim*
		1956	Invasion of Suez	1956	Osborne's *Look Back in Anger*
1957	Treaty of Rome				
1958	De Gaulle President of France	1959	First motorway		
1962	Cuban Missile Crisis			1962	Coventry Cathedral consecrated
1963	Kennedy assassinated				
1963	Vietnam War begins				
1966	Chinese Cultural Revolution begins				
1967	Six-Day War				
1968	Russian invasion of Czechoslovakia				
1969	First man on Moon	1973	Joined European Common Market	1976	Lasdun's National Theatre
1979	Afghanistan war begins	1974	Miners' strike		
		1980	Self–sufficiency in North Sea oil		
1980	Iran–Iraq war begins	1982	Falklands War		
		1983	Conservatives re-elected under Margaret Thatcher	1983	Burrell Collection Museum, Glasgow opened
				1983	William Golding wins Nobel Prize for Literature
1985	Gorbachev assumes power in USSR	1987	Thatcher wins third term of office	1986	Richard Rogers's Lloyds of London
1989	Tiananmen Square massacre	1990	Thatcher resigns; John Major becomes Prime Minister		
1989	Berlin Wall pulled down				
1990	Iraq invades Kuwait			1991	Tim Berners-Lee, World Wide Web
1991	Gulf War				

World	Britain – Political	Culture
		1991 Helen Sharman, first British astronaut
1992 Maastricht Treaty creates the European Union	1992 John Major wins general election	1992 Damien Hirst, *The Physical Impossibility of Death in the Mind of Someone Living*
	1992 Britain leaves the Exchange Rate Mechanism	1992 Premier League
	1992 Channel Tunnel opens	
	1992 Omagh bombed by Provisional IRA	1993 Irvine Welsh, *Trainspotting*
	1994 Church of England ordains women priests	
1995 Balkans War		
	1996 Dunblane Massacre	1996 Dolly the Sheep
	1996 BSE Crisis	
	1997 Labour win the general election under Tony Blair	1997 J.K. Rowling, *Harry Potter and the Philosopher's Stone*
1997 Hong Kong handed back to China	1997 Death of Princess Diana	1997 'Sensation' exhibition
		1997 Colin St John Wilson, British Library reading room
	1998 Good Friday Agreement	
	1999 Scottish Parliament opens at Holyrood	
1999 Launch of the Euro		
		2000 Norman Foster, Millennium Bridge
		2000 Tate Modern
		2000 First series of Big Brother
		2000 Zadie Smith, *White Teeth*
2001 September 11 attacks in United States	2001 Labour relected in general election	
2001 Coalition invasion of Afghanistan		
2002 Bali Bombing		2002 Golden Jubilee
2003 Invasion of Iraq		2003 Twenty20 cricket begins
2004 Indian Ocean Tsunami		2004 Norman Foster, 30 St Mary Axe (The Gherkin)
		2004 Alan Bennett, *The History Boys*
2005 Hurricane Katrina, United States	2005 Civil partnerships introduced	
	2005 July 7 bombings in London	
	2005 Labour re-elected for a third time	
	2005 IRA ends its armed campaign	2006 Richard Dawkins, *The God Delusion*
	2007 Gordon Brown succeeds Tony Blair as prime minister	
2008 Barack Obama becomes US president		
2008 Global banking crisis		
	2009 MPs' expenses scandal	2010 Rise of social media
2010 Haiti earthquake	2010 Hung Parliament in general election	
2010 BP oil spill, Mexican Gulf		
2010 Arab Spring begins		
2011 Queen Elizabeth II visits the Republic of Ireland	2011 Prince William marries Catherine Middleton	
2011 British troops leave Iraq		
2011 Death of Osama bin Laden		
2011 International intervention in Libya		2012 London Olympics
		2013 Renzo Piano, The Shard
2013 British troops leave Afghanistan		2014 Paul Cummins and Tom Piper, *Blood Swept Lands and Seas of Red*
	2014 Scotland rejects independence in a referendum	
2015 Extremist attacks in Paris		2015 Banksy, *Dismaland*
	2015 Conservative Party wins general election	
	2016 European referendum in Britain	

Prime Ministers

Reign of King George II — 1727–1760

1727	Robert Walpole
1741	Earl of Wilmington
1743	Henry Pelham
1754	Duke of Newcastle
1756	Duke of Devonshire
1757	Duke of Newcastle

Reign of King George III — 1760–1820

1760	Duke of Newcastle
1762	Earl of Bute
1763	George Grenville
1765	Marquess of Rockingham
1766	Earl of Chatham
1768	Duke of Grafton
1770	Lord North
1782	Marquess of Rockingham *27 March*
1782	Earl of Shelburne *4 July*
1783	Duke of Portland *2 April*
1783	William Pitt (the Younger) *19 December*
1801	Henry Addington
1804	William Pitt
1806	William Wyndham Grenville
1807	Duke of Portland
1809	Spencer Perceval
1812	Earl of Liverpool

Reign of King George IV — 1820–1830

1820	Earl of Liverpool (Tory)
1827	George Canning (Tory coalition) *10 April*
1827	Viscount Goderich (Tory) *31 August*
1828	Duke of Wellington (Tory)

Reign of King William IV — 1830–1837

1830	Duke of Wellington (Tory)
1830	Earl Grey (Whig) *22 November*
1830	Viscount Melbourne (Whig) *16 July*
1834	Duke of Wellington (Tory) *17 November*
1834	Robert Peel (Tory) *10 December*
1835	Viscount Melbourne (Whig)

Reign of Queen Victoria (1837–1901)

1837	Viscount Melbourne (Whig)
1841	Robert Peel (Tory)
1846	Lord John Russell (Whig)
1852	Earl of Derby (Tory) *23 February*
1852	Earl of Aberdeen (Tory Coalition) *19 December*

1855	Viscount Palmerston (Liberal)
1858	Earl of Derby (Conservative)
1859	Viscount Palmerston (Liberal)
1865	Earl Russell (Liberal)
1866	Earl of Derby (Conservative)
1868	Benjamin Disraeli (Conservative) *27 February*
1868	William Ewart Gladstone (Liberal) *3 December*
1874	Benjamin Disraeli (Conservative)
1880	William Ewart Gladstone (Liberal)
1885	Marquess of Salisbury (Conservative)
1886	William Ewart Gladstone (Liberal) *1 February*
1886	Marquess of Salisbury (Conservative) *25 July*
1892	William Ewart Gladstone (Liberal)
1894	Earl of Rosebery (Liberal)
1895	Marquess of Salisbury

Reign of Edward VII (1901–1910)

1901	Marquess of Salisbury (Conservative)
1902	Arthur James Balfour (Conservative)
1905	Henry Campbell–Bannerman (Liberal)
1908	Herbert Henry Asquith (Liberal)

Reign of King George V — 1910–1936

1910	Herbert Henry Asquith (Liberal coalition from May 1915)
1916	David Lloyd George (Liberal coalition)
1922	Andrew Bonar Law (Conservative)
1923	Stanley Baldwin (Conservative)
1924	James Ramsay MacDonald (Labour) *27 January*
1924	Stanley Baldwin (Conservative) *4 November*
1929	James Ramsay MacDonald (Labour coalition from 1931)
1935	Stanley Baldwin (Conservative)

Reign of King Edward VIII (1936)

1936	Stanley Baldwin (Conservative)

Reign of King George VI — 1936–1952

1936	Stanley Baldwin (Conservative)
1937	Neville Chamberlain (Conservative)
1940	Winston Churchill (Coalition)
1945	Clement Attlee (Labour)
1951	Winston Churchill (Conservative)

Reign of Elizabeth II — 1952–

1952	Winston Churchill (Conservative)
1955	Anthony Eden (Conservative)
1957	Harold Macmillan (Conservative)
1963	Alec Douglas Hone (Conservative)
1974	Harold Wilson (Labour)
1970	Edward Heath (Conservative)
1974	Harold Wilson (Labour)
1976	James Callaghan (Labour)
1979	Margaret Thatcher (Conservative)
1990	John Major (Conservative)
1997	Tony Blair (Labour)
2007	Gordon Brown (Labour)
2010	David Cameron (Coalition)
2015	David Cameron (Conservative)

Leaders of the Opposition since the Ministers of the Crown Act 1937

1937–45	Clement Attlee
1945–51	Winston Churchill
1951–55	Clement Attlee
1955–63	Hugh Gaitskell
1963–64	Harold Wilson
1965–70	Edward Heath
1970–74	Harold Wilson
1974–75	Edward Heath
1975–79	Margaret Thatcher
1980–83	Michael Foot
1983–92	Neil Kinnock
1992–94	John Smith
1994–97	Tony Blair
1997	John Major
1997–2001	William Hague
2001–03	Iain Duncan Smith
2003–05	Michael Howard
2010–15	Ed Miliband
2015–	Jeremy Corbyn

Index

Index

Index

Index

Index

Bibliographical Note

Perhaps the best of the one-volume histories of
England which cover the ground more fully than
this book has room to do is *The Oxford Illustrated
History of Britain* (ed. Kenneth O. Morgan, 1984).
Others that can be recommended are R. J. White's
A Short History of England (revised edition, 1962),
Paul Johnson's *A History of the English People*
(revised edition, 1985), Jasper Ridley's *A History
of England* (1950), E. L. Woodward's *A History of
England* (third edition, 1965) and Hugh Kearney's
The British Isles: A History of Four Nations (1989).
Classic older works are Lord Macaulay's *History
of England* (paperback edition, 1986) and
G. M. Trevelyan's *A Shortened History of England*
(paperback edition, 1987).

Three good generously illustrated books
are F. E. Halliday's *A Concise History of England*
(revised edition, 1980), John Burke's *An Illustrated
History of England* (new edition, 1985), and David
McDowell's *An Illustrated History of Britain* (1989).

Three social histories are Maurice Ashley's
The People of England (1982), Asa Briggs's *A Social
History of England* (1983) and my own *The English:
A Social History: 1066–1945* (1987). Christopher
Taylor has revised W. G. Hoskins's *The Making of
the English Landscape* (1988).

For more detailed treatment, there is the
splendid fifteen-volume *Oxford History of England*
of which the first volume, *A Polite and Commercial
People: England 1727–1783*, appeared in 1989.

Christopher Hibbert, 1992

Phaidon Press Ltd.
Regent's Wharf
All Saints Street
London, N1 9PA

Phaidon Press Inc.
65 Bleecker Street
New York, NY 10012

phaidon.com

First edition published 1992
Illustrated edition published 2016
© 2016 Phaidon Press
Text © 1992 Christopher Hibbert
Illustrations © 2016 John Broadley
New chapter text by Seán Lang

A CIP catalogue record of this book is available from
the British Library.

All rights reserved. No part of this publication may be
reproduced, stored in a retrieval system or transmitted
in any form or by any means, electronic, mechanical,
photocopying, recording or otherwise, without prior
permission of Phaidon Press.

Designed by Hyperkit

Printed in China

Commissioning editor: Victoria Clarke
Project editor: Ellen Christie
Production controller: Rebecca Price

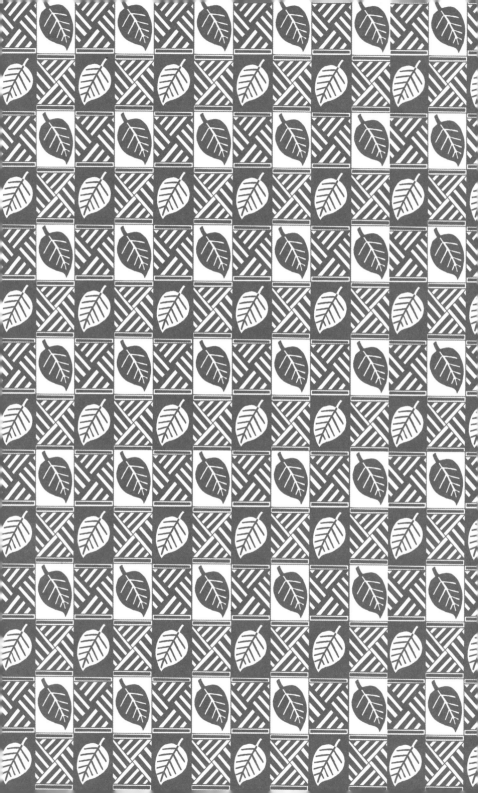